THE
SUGAR HOUSE

Alana Valentine

Currency Press,
Sydney

CURRENT THEATRE SERIES

First published in 2018
by Currency Press Pty Ltd,
PO Box 2287, Strawberry Hills, NSW, 2012, Australia
enquiries@currency.com.au
www.currency.com.au
in association with Belvoir, Sydney.

Copyright: *The Sugar House* © Alana Valentine, 2018.

COPYING FOR EDUCATIONAL PURPOSES
The Australian *Copyright Act 1968* (Act) allows a maximum of one chapter or 10% of this book, whichever is the greater, to be copied by any educational institution for its educational purposes provided that that educational institution (or the body that administers it) has given a remuneration notice to Copyright Agency (CA) under the Act.
For details of the CA licence for educational institutions contact CA, 11/66 Goulburn Street, Sydney, NSW, 2000; tel: within Australia 1800 066 844 toll free; outside Australia 61 2 9394 7600; fax: 61 2 9394 7601; email: info@copyright.com.au

COPYING FOR OTHER PURPOSES
Except as permitted under the Act, for example a fair dealing for the purposes of study, research, criticism or review, no part of this book may be reproduced, stored in a retrieval system, or transmitted in any form or by any means without prior written permission. All enquiries should be made to the publisher at the address above.

Any performance or public reading of *The Sugar House* is forbidden unless a licence has been received from the author or the author's agent. The purchase of this book in no way gives the purchaser the right to perform the play in public, whether by means of a staged production or a reading. All applications for public performance should be addressed to Creative Representation, PO Box 208, Surry Hills NSW 2010, Australia; ph: 61 2 9690 5900; fax: 61 2 9690 0980; email: admin@creativerep.com.au

Typeset by Dean Nottle for Currency Press.
Cover design: Alphabet Studio.

A catalogue record for this book is available from the National Library of Australia

Contents

THE SUGAR HOUSE

    Act One   1

    Act Two   55

Theatre Program at the end of the playtext

Currency Press acknowledges the Traditional Owners of the Country on which we live and work. We pay our respects to all Aboriginal and Torres Strait Islander Elders, past and present.

For my uncle Ross Wainwright.

The Sugar House was first produced by Belvoir at Belvoir St Theatre, Sydney, on 9 May 2018, with the following cast:

NARELLE MACREADIE	Sheridan Harbridge
MARGO MACREADIE	Sacha Horler
SIDNEY MACREADIE / CONSTABLE RUPERT / BRIAN TUCKAN / TERENCE SHEAHAN	Lex Marinos
OLLIE MACREADIE / ZEE	Josh McConville
JUNE MACREADIE	Kris McQuade
JENNY/PRIN	Nikki Shiels

Director, Sarah Goodes
Set Designer, Michael Hankin
Costume Designer, Emma Vine
Lighting Designer, Damien Cooper
Composer, Steve Francis
Sound Designer, Michael Toisuta
Stage Manager, Isabella Kerdijk
Assistant Stage Manager, Keiren Smith
Stage Management Secondment, Ella Griffin

The author would like to thank Terry Sheahan, NSW Attorney General in 1985, who generously agreed to be interviewed for this work, members of the Pyrmont History Group, long-time Pyrmont local Jennice Kersh, Shirley Fitzgerald and Tim Peach, and Mitchell Librarian Helen Benacek.

The 'Bee-Boy's Song' (pages 10–11) is by Rudyard Kipling.

CHARACTERS

JUNE MACREADIE
NARELLE MACREADIE, her granddaughter
MARGO MACREADIE, her daughter
SIDNEY MACREADIE, her husband
OLLIE (OLIVER) MACREADIE, her son
JENNY, Ollie's girlfriend/wife
PRIN, a real estate agent
CONSTABLE RUPERT, a police officer
BRIAN TUSKAN, state MP
SHEAHAN, NSW Attorney General
STEWART, a doctor
ZEE, a tattoo artist

Roles are distributed amongst six actors as follows:

JUNE MACREADIE
NARELLE
MARGO
SIDNEY / CONSTABLE RUPERT / BRIAN TUSKAN / SHEAHAN / STEWART
OLLIE / ZEE
JENNY / PRIN

SETTING

A Jacksons Landing apartment in Pyrmont in 2007—which transforms to the CSR Refinery and various other locations in 1966/1967 including the Macreadie Pyrmont home in John Street, an MP office in a School of Arts building and a police station, then to various locations in 1985, including homes, the foyer of the Goodsell Building in Sydney, a tattoo parlour, and a police station—before returning finally to 2007.

This play went to press before the end of rehearsals and may differ from the play as performed.

ACT ONE

SCENE ONE

2007.

NARELLE *is being shown around an apartment by a real estate agent,* PRIN.

PRIN: The penthouse has three bedrooms, and an incredible view.
NARELLE: So I see.
PRIN: Many of the Jacksons Landing apartments have bathtubs, balconies, and built-ins.
NARELLE: Yes.
PRIN: And of course there is the extensive landscaping and Sydney harbourside promenades. Do you have a dog?
NARELLE: No.
PRIN: Well, if you do decide to get one, they're completely welcome.
NARELLE: There are a lot of people with dogs then?
PRIN: Well. Some. But not big dogs.

   Beat.

   A lot of the residents are empty-nesters, people in their fifties who no longer want the maintenance demands of a suburban garden. On Tuesdays they have aquarobics in the Glasshouse Pool.

   NARELLE *nods and looks around.*

NARELLE: I saw an old sign, Cane-ite, on the side of the building.
PRIN: The Jacksons Landing developers are committed to maintaining the heritage of the site and a series of interpretive installations and salvaged relics throughout the development commemorate the area's history.
NARELLE: So then who is Mr Jackson?
PRIN: Mr Jackson?
NARELLE: Of Jacksons Landing?
PRIN: Oh. [*Laughing*] I don't know. It would be somebody ... historic.
NARELLE: Somebody who landed ... somewhere.
PRIN: Nearby.

They both laugh now.

NARELLE: Perhaps where the Jackson Five came ashore on their world tour.

PRIN: Could be.

Beat.

Are you especially looking in Pyrmont?

NARELLE: Yes, I wanted to be close to …

PRIN: The water?

NARELLE: [*lying*] Yes.

PRIN: Max Dupain was commissioned to photograph the site for the CSR in the sixties.

NARELLE: Yes.

PRIN: There was a sugar refinery on this site for many years. I don't always mention it since some people are concerned about industrial waste even though there is absolutely none of that.

NARELLE: Good.

PRIN: It was a pretty scungy area but they've cleaned it up. Changed the character of the place.

NARELLE: The character?

PRIN: Big Chinese community of course.

NARELLE: From the Haymarket?

PRIN: For the casino.

NARELLE smiles.

But there are people here from all over the world.

NARELLE: Money being very culturally diverse.

PRIN's mobile phone rings.

PRIN: Excuse me. [*Into the phone*] Could you give me half an hour? Alright. Tell them I'll be there in ten minutes.

She hangs up.

I'm sorry, Ms Macreadie? I have to leave to meet another client who wants to settle immediately.

NARELLE: Oh. Well, could I …?

PRIN: I … I could meet you back here later. No, actually I've got another open house. Tomorrow?

NARELLE: Why don't I just pull the door after me.

Pause.

PRIN: It's actually a legal thing. Legally I can't leave you alone in the apartment.

NARELLE: Yes, but are you a letter-of-the-law or a spirit-of-the-law kind of person, Prin?

PRIN: I'm a real estate agent, I just need you to leave.

Pause.

NARELLE: A constant refrain.

PRIN: Sorry?

NARELLE: A constant refrain for the people of Pyrmont.

PRIN: Look, I just have another client.

They begin to leave.

NARELLE: Only, I think I left my umbrella in the other room. I'll just go …

PRIN: [*with a sigh*] The toilets are not connected yet.

NARELLE: Okay.

PRIN: So please don't use them.

NARELLE: No.

PRIN: Really, I've asked people before not to use them and then the builder comes in the next day to a nasty little surprise.

NARELLE: Yes, I can see that's what it would be.

PRIN: People who you would never think would do such a thing.

NARELLE: I won't use the toilet.

PRIN: Please don't. I'll send security to follow up.

PRIN *leaves.*

NARELLE *walks around.*

Out of the walls, the past pours out. The noise and steam and industry of the CSR site becomes deafening as NARELLE *is thrown back to her childhood.*

SCENE TWO

December, 1966.

SIDNEY MACREADIE, *Narelle's grandfather, enters and continues to open cupboards, transform furniture and re-create the CSR site. He grabs* NARELLE*'s hand and jerks her to her feet.*

SID: First they squeeze out all the juice with the roller mills and let it cool. Then it passes through those big vats you saw, which have got the slake lime in them. That gets rid of all the dirt.
NARELLE: How can there still be dirt in it?
SID: That sugar is full of dirt, that's why we have to refine it.
NARELLE: And is that like to clean it?
SID: That gets out all the impurities.
NARELLE: But do you actually make the sugar, Poppa?
SID: I maintain the machines that make the sugar.

They keep walking.

NARELLE: What do you have to do to the machines?
SID: I have to fix them if they break down.
NARELLE: Does the sugar ever spill out all over the floor?
SID: All over the floor?
NARELLE: Yeah?
SID: It's not supposed to. But it sometimes does.
NARELLE: And then what do you do?
SID: I have to stop the machine to fix it. Like now.

The noise and din of the factory stops.

NARELLE: What can I do?
SID: Just sit quietly for Poppa.

NARELLE *sits and then gets up. She is holding a newspaper.*

So what's in the news then?
NARELLE: [*reading*] 'Ryan claims guard shot at him first.'
SID: Does he now?
NARELLE: [*reading*] 'Ronald Gregory Ryan, who has been sentenced to hang for the murder of prison guard Michael Martin, claims that it was a stray bullet from the rifle of another guard, Frank Flower, which [*hesitating*] ricocheted to kill the victim.'
SID: Well, he would say that, wouldn't he?
NARELLE: Don't you believe him, Poppa?
SID: I'm not saying I don't believe him.
NARELLE: Why not?
SID: Because your grandmother would have my guts for garters if I did.
NARELLE: What are garters?
SID: Just keep reading, Doll.

ACT ONE

NARELLE: [*reading*] 'Critics of the Victorian premier are accusing him of conducting an irrational vendetta against Ryan.'
SID: A what?
NARELLE: A vendetta. It means when you don't like someone just because they're them rather than having a proper reason.
SID: Like a grudge.
NARELLE: Yeah. But if you're important enough you don't have to have grudges because you can have vendettas.
SID: Out of the mouths of babes.
NARELLE: What?
SID: What you say is very smart.
NARELLE: So why don't you believe him?

Pause.

SID: Maybe it was a ricocheting bullet. Maybe it wasn't. Truth is, he shouldn't have been trying to escape and he shouldn't have been shooting at the guards.
NARELLE: Nanna says that's no reason to kill a man.
SID: And she's right about that.
NARELLE: Nanna says the State hides behind the lawyers but it's really just cold-blooded murder.
SID: Throw that paper away now. Let's stop talking about it.

NARELLE *looks up from the paper.*

NARELLE: What's bad blood?
SID: What did I say about that paper?
NARELLE: But what is it?
SID: Somethin' you can't do nothin' about.

SID *grabs the paper and puts it in a garbage bin.*

NARELLE: Don't just put it in the bin. Somebody might want to read it.
SID: [*with a laugh*] Not much point doing that.
NARELLE: Why?

SID *takes both her hands in his.*

SID: None of this lot can read, Doll.
NARELLE: Why not?
SID: They never learned.

NARELLE *stares.*

NARELLE: Is that because they have bad blood?
SID: No.
NARELLE: Then what is it?
SID: Some people think that if people go off the rails and get caught doing things they're not supposed to it's because of something born in them. Something they can't control.
NARELLE: Is that true?
SID: I don't know, Doll.
NARELLE: The paper says Ronald Ryan has bad blood.
SID: I don't know about that, love. He has a bloody unlucky streak, though.
NARELLE: I'm going to ask Nanna.
SID: No, Doll.
NARELLE: What?
SID: Promise me you won't ask your Nanna about bad blood.
NARELLE: Why?
SID: Do you promise?

Pause.

NARELLE: No.
SID: Okay. Well, I guess I'll just have to leave you here instead of going home.
NARELLE: Leave me here? Forever?
SID: Yep.
NARELLE: Okay. I promise.

Pause.

Can I ask Mum?
SID: I told you what it is. Why do you need to ask anyone?
NARELLE: You don't tell me some things even though I'm eight.
SID: Does your mum tell you secret things now that you're eight?
NARELLE: Nanna says Mum should shut her trap around the puppy.
SID: Really? When did we get a dog?
NARELLE: No, Poppa. That's me. Shut her trap around me.
SID: Yeah, well, you do smell a bit woofy.
NARELLE: Do not.

He growls. She giggles. He barks, she laughs. He exits.

ACT ONE

NARELLE *opens a drawer and finds a child's exercise book and pens. She spreads them out on the floor and begins to do her homework.*

SCENE THREE

June and Sid's home.

JUNE MACREADIE *enters with a cotton tablecloth and snaps it in the air before throwing it over a table.* NARELLE *continues with her homework.*

JUNE: Come sit up at the table when you're writing, Doll.
NARELLE: I'm alright on the floor, Nanna.
JUNE: You want people to say I can't afford a set of chairs?
NARELLE: No.
JUNE: Then come and sit up when I tell you.

    NARELLE *moves her things.*

NARELLE: How do you spell 'career', Nanna?
JUNE: C.A.R.E ...

    Pause.

A ... No, not a. Just use spin instead.
NARELLE: Spin?
JUNE: You can career out of control or you can spin out of control.
NARELLE: Not for driving.
JUNE: Then use belt. You career down a hill or you belt down a hill.
NARELLE: For what you want to do with your life. Your career.
JUNE: Oh. Your career.
NARELLE: That's our homework. To write what we want to do for a career.
JUNE: Now I got ya.
NARELLE: What should I put?
JUNE: Well, you should put what you want to do when you grow up.
NARELLE: I don't know.
JUNE: Well, have a think.
NARELLE: What sort of thing is a career?
JUNE: Well, it's your job, I guess.
NARELLE: Like Poppa, working at the sugar factory all his life. Is that his career?

JUNE: Put it like this. You know that big house at the end of John Street?
NARELLE: Where the refinery boss lives?
JUNE: Yeah. He has a career whereas Poppa has a job.
NARELLE: What's the difference?
JUNE: Well, what do you think is the difference?
NARELLE: His house is bigger.
JUNE: That's right.
NARELLE: But he still has to put up with the smell when the incinerator starts up. Poo. And when they're cooking the molasses. Pee-you. Rotten egg gas.
JUNE: And the sour smell of milk from the dairies and the sewerage from Blackwattle Creek and the offal from the abattoirs.
NARELLE: None of that's here anymore, Nanna.
JUNE: Yeah, I know, funny how I can still smell it, though.
NARELLE: Nanna.
JUNE: What?
NARELLE: If that refinery boss has to to smell all that like us, what's the use of having a career?
JUNE: You know that green mould we have all on the walls?
NARELLE: Yeah.
JUNE: He doesn't have that.
NARELLE: But we find faces in that mould.
JUNE: Well, you know that leak we have in our roof?
NARELLE: Yeah.
JUNE: He doesn't have that.
NARELLE: But we use the water to clean our dishes.
JUNE: Okay, but he doesn't have to go outside when he wants to go to the toilet.
NARELLE: Well, where does he go?
JUNE: He has a special room inside his house with his toilet inside.

    NARELLE *is wide-eyed.*

NARELLE: But doesn't that just add to all the bad smells?
JUNE: Just put what you want to be for your homework.
NARELLE: Well, what do you want me to be?
JUNE: I don't care what you do, my love, as long as you stay out of jail.
NARELLE: I can't put that.
JUNE: Why not?

ACT ONE

NARELLE: That's not a ambition.
JUNE: It is, in my books, my love.
NARELLE: No, that's just a threat. For people who are bad.
JUNE: Or get on the wrong side of a corrupt cop.
NARELLE: What?
JUNE: Nothing. Don't put that down.
NARELLE: What makes you think I'm going to go to jail?

> JUNE *comes over and hugs her.*

JUNE: You? You're not going to jail. You're the sugar in my tea.
NARELLE: Can I put that?
JUNE: What?
NARELLE: I want to grow up and be the sugar in my nanna's tea?

> JUNE *hugs her.* MARGO, *Narelle's mother, enters.*

JUNE: You're late.
MARGO: I was busy trying to save my marriage.
JUNE: Don't tell me that. You said he was the one.
MARGO: Apparently I'm the only one who still thinks so.

> JUNE *begins packing up Narelle's things.*

JUNE: You don't get the luxury of a crisis in your marriage, Margo.
MARGO: The luxury?
JUNE: That's right, the luxury. You find a way to make it work, you find a way to make it last, and you do it because you don't have any other choice.
MARGO: You think I want this to be happening?
JUNE: I think you want the excitement.
MARGO: I do not.
JUNE: Then you want to be happy.

> MARGO *looks at her.*

MARGO: I should just be unhappy?
JUNE: You should be filthy bloody miserable and you should get used to it because that is what life is.
MARGO: I'm trying.
JUNE: You're not trying. You're uncomfortable with being unhappy because you think it's going to end.
MARGO: We just need a break.

JUNE: No.
MARGO: Just a couple of days.
JUNE: No.
MARGO: Mum, I'll really try. I'll make peace with unhappy. But I can't have Narelle in the middle of it. Even you don't want that.
JUNE: I can't look after her.
MARGO: No, I'll come too. Just for a couple of days.

> JUNE *looks at her and then sees* SID *entering.*

I'll ask Dad.

> SID *has been stung by a bee. He is attended by* MARGO.

JUNE: What's wrong with you?
SID: Bloody little thing.
NARELLE: Was there a bee caught in your clothes again, Poppa?
SID: Can't work with sugar and not attract bees. They're always hanging around when you go up the pay office there. Trying to sting you for a quid like everyone else, eh?
NARELLE: How many times is that?
SID: What?
NARELLE: That you've been stung.
SID: I don't know.
MARGO: 'Course he does.
SID: It'd be in the hundreds.
NARELLE: How many hundred?
SID: I don't know.
NARELLE: I thought they took bets.
JUNE: How do you know about that?
NARELLE: Everyone knows about that. They take bets on how many times you've been stung before you become immune and it doesn't hurt anymore.
JUNE: You should get on with your homework, sweetheart.
NARELLE: But are we staying here for a couple of days?
MARGO: Is that alright?
SID: That'd be lovely.

> [*Singing*] Fly away—die away—
> Dwindle down and leave you!
> But if you don't deceive your bees,
> Your bees will not deceive you.

SID *swoons a bit.*

Sing with me, Doll.

NARELLE & SID: [*singing together*]
Don't you wait where the trees are,
When the lightning's at play,
Nor don't you hate where bees are,
Or else they'll pine away.

Pine away—dwine away—
Anything to leave you!
But if you never grieve your bees,
Your bees'll never grieve you.

MARGO: Are you alright, Dad?
SID: Nothing a cold beer and a little lie-down won't fix.

SID *sits in a chair on one side of the stage as* MARGO *goes off to get him a beer.*

JUNE *and* NARELLE *go back to the table.* NARELLE *continues with her homework.* JUNE *is shelling peas.*

NARELLE: Nanna, is Mummy alright?
JUNE: Of course she is.
NARELLE: Are her and Daddy breaking up?
JUNE: Of course not. Do your homework.
NARELLE: I can't.
JUNE: Why not?
NARELLE: It's Maths. Percentages.
JUNE: Oh, percentages.
NARELLE: Maths is stupid.
JUNE: No, it's not. You love Maths. And you're good at it.
NARELLE: Am not.
JUNE: You use it all the time.
NARELLE: When?
JUNE: Say I get you to go along to the bookie and put a bet on a horse for me at two-to-one. What does that mean?
NARELLE: That means if you win you'll get twice what you put on.
JUNE: That's Maths.
NARELLE: Yeah, but everyone knows that.

JUNE: Then what if that horse is at six-to-four for a win and eight-to-three for a place.
NARELLE: And how much have you put on?
JUNE: Three dollars.
NARELLE: [*working it out on her page*] Then you'd get seven dollars fifty for a win and five dollars for a place.
JUNE: Good. Now what if I put a dollar on for a trifecta?
NARELLE: At what odds?
JUNE: Seven-to-three for a win and six-to-two for a place.

    NARELLE *does some calculations.*

NARELLE: Then you'd get three dollars thirty-three for a win and one dollar seventy-five for a place.
JUNE: See how good you are at Maths?
NARELLE: But these are not odds. They're percentages.
JUNE: So convert them into odds. Imagine that you're going back to collect my winnings.

    NARELLE *does some calculations.*

NARELLE: Hey, that's really great. Thanks, Nanna.
JUNE: That's my pleasure, my darling.

    NARELLE *does some more calculations.*

NARELLE: Hey, Nanna.
JUNE: Yeah?
NARELLE: What odds would you give on Mum and Dad?

    JUNE *looks at her.*

JUNE: Eight-to-one that it won't last out the year.

    There is a sound of a car outside.

Look out, here's trouble.

    June and Sid's son, OLLIE, *enters. He is wearing a woman's dress. The woman with him,* JENNY, *is wearing a white sheet, wrapped around her body.*

    JUNE, SID, *and* NARELLE *stare at them in disbelief.*

Trust me, I don't want to know.
OLLIE: It was the bloody cops.

JUNE: Ollie, unless you're intending to go around like that for the duration, I suggest you get changed and we'll never mention it again.

MARGO *enters, carrying a beer.*

JENNY: Hi, I'm Jenny.
MARGO: Jenny Wren, who he fished out of a shallow birdbath.
OLLIE: The coppers stopped me just outside the Terminus.
JENNY: They did.
OLLIE: For no reason. Driving down Harris Street, about to turn into John Street, minding my own business.
JUNE: Dressed up like a Christmas tree at Easter.
MARGO: Dressed up like Brutus at a Roman toga party.
OLLIE: I wasn't wearing this.
JENNY: No, he wasn't. I was wearing that.
SID: Come on, you're scaring the pup.
NARELLE: No he's not. What were you wearing?
MARGO: Your uncle was wearing the sheet.
NARELLE: How come?
MARGO: Because he thinks he's Jesus Christ and can't stop rising from the dead.
JENNY: He sure can rise again and again.
JUNE: Not in front of the child, if you don't mind.
OLLIE: Listen. Jenny washed me strides. And me shirt. So I pulled the sheet off the bed and wrapped it around me.
NARELLE: Whose sheet?
JUNE: Never mind.
SID: Well, get on with the story, Moses, what did the cops want?
OLLIE: We were just going down the shops for a beer.
MARGO: You were gonna go in a pub like that?
JENNY: I was going to go in and buy a couple of bottles.
NARELLE: While Ollie waited in the car.
OLLIE: Take the prize as my favourite niece.
NARELLE: I'm your only niece.
JUNE: And I've only got so many more years to live, so if you must persist with this story could you bloody get on with it?
OLLIE: I'm driving.
MARGO: Dressed as Lawrence of Arabia.

OLLIE: We've picked up the beer and we're driving home.
MARGO: With Miss Keg On Legs in the passenger seat.
OLLIE: And the cops flag me down. For no reason. For absolutely no reason. And when they see what I've got on they tell me I can't drive dressed in a sheet. So I tell Jenny to give me her clothes. Jenny gets out of the car, takes off her dress and hands it to me. I remove the sheet …
JENNY: And they had a good look at his rod and tackle too.
NARELLE: At what?
OLLIE: I remove the sheet and Jenny wraps it around herself.
MARGO: You're a bloody genius.
OLLIE: No. I am. I am. Because the cops were so entertained by this little show. So entertained that they didn't give me a ticket.
JENNY: Isn't that great?
JUNE: I don't know who's more of an idiot. Him for asking you to strip in front of two leering coppers or you for agreeing to it.
JENNY: Well, it got him off, didn't it?
JUNE: Come and have your bath, Narelle.
NARELLE: I want to hear what happened next.
MARGO: Go with your grandmother and have a bath and then straight to bed.
OLLIE: If she's here with the pup, where am I supposed to sleep?
MARGO: It's still half my room.
OLLIE: Not since you moved in with boofhead it's not.
SID: Shut up, the both of you. Margo and Narelle are in the room, you and Julie are on the divan.
JUNE: You got one sheet you can use, there's another out in the laundry.
SID: Now get out of them clothes, Ollie. You look ridiculous.

They all exit except for OLLIE *and* JENNY.

JENNY: Tell me one thing.
OLLIE: Sure, babe.
JENNY: Why did we have to come here?
OLLIE: Well, I had to get some clothes, didn't I?
JENNY: But you must have known they'd have a go.
OLLIE: A go? That wasn't a go.
JENNY: Then what was it?
OLLIE: That was them bein' nice.

JENNY: Nice? Your mother's a bit of a witch.
OLLIE: Oi.
JENNY: What?
OLLIE: You want to stay here the night, you'll take that back.
JENNY: Well, I don't know if I do want to stay here the night, if that's what they're going to be like.
OLLIE: Do you have a mother?
JENNY: Yeah.
OLLIE: Would she take the food out of her own mouth and put it in yours?
JENNY: I humiliated myself for you.
OLLIE: And look what you get in return.

Pause.

JENNY: Why do you really want to stay here?
OLLIE: I told ya.
JENNY: What's with you and the cops?

Pause.

OLLIE: There's just never nothin' in yer fridge. That's why I wanted to come here.
JENNY: You've only known me two weeks.
OLLIE: Yeah. Which is how I know how cold and ungiving your Kelvinator is.

Beat.

But you have other warm spots.

He slaps her on the backside as they exit.

SCENE FOUR

Tendrils of smoke sneak onto the stage. MARGO *and* NARELLE *are asleep.*
NARELLE *begins coughing from the smoke that is building in the room.*

NARELLE: Mum! Mum, wake up. Mum! *Mum!*

She gets out of bed and goes over to her mother, trying to wake her.

Mum. Wake up. Please wake up. Nanna. *Nanna!*

JUNE *enters, panicked.*

JUNE: Get away from the bed.

NARELLE: What do you want me to do?
JUNE: Get out.

> SID *is close behind* JUNE. *He shakes* MARGO *violently, jolting her out of bed.*

SID: Wake up, Margo.
MARGO: What?
SID: Wake up. You've set the bloody bed on fire.
MARGO: I haven't done anything.
JUNE: Get up, you stupid girl, or you'll burn the bloody house down.
MARGO: Stop telling me what to do.
JUNE: Get out of the way.

> JUNE *and* SID *lift the mattress which is smouldering on one end. They carry it past the horrified* NARELLE *and still dopey* MARGO.

NARELLE: The mattress was on fire.
MARGO: Yeah, well, they got it in time.
NARELLE: How did it catch alight?
MARGO: I don't need my own daughter nagging at me, alright?
NARELLE: Alright.
MARGO: I'm going to cop an earful from your nan, so I don't need it from you, do I?
NARELLE: No.
MARGO: Get back into bed.
NARELLE: But it's all smoky.
MARGO: I said, get back into bed.

> NARELLE *gets back into bed. Suddenly there is a loud knock at the front door.*

Mum! Mum!
JUNE: [*offstage*] What?
MARGO: Someone is knocking at the front door.

> JUNE *comes back in.*

JUNE: Well, answer it, for Christ's sake. It'll just be the neighbours wanting to complain.
MARGO: I don't want to have to talk to the neighbours.
JUNE: Don't smoke in bed before you go to sleep and you won't have to.

> *There is another loud knock at the front door.*

Tell them it's under control.

> CONSTABLE RUPERT *enters.*

RUPERT: Good evening.
MARGO: God help me, it was just a bit of smoke.
RUPERT: I beg your pardon?
MARGO: Where'd you come from? None of this lot round here would have copper'd on us, I know that for a fact.
RUPERT: Are you the lady of the house?
MARGO: It's all under control, alright? Just a little bit of smoke and it's all under control.

> JUNE *appears at the door.*

JUNE: As my daughter says, sir, it was just a little accident with a candle.
RUPERT: Mrs Macreadie, is your son Oliver Macreadie in residence with you at present?
JUNE: I don't understand.
RUPERT: May I speak to your son Oliver Macreadie?
MARGO: He didn't have anything to do with it.
RUPERT: With what?
JUNE: He's not here.
RUPERT: He has you listed as his place of residence.
JUNE: Yeah, well he's not here.
RUPERT: His car's out front.
JUNE: He lent it to his sister to move her things.
RUPERT: From where?
MARGO: I've left my husband.
NARELLE: Why have we left Daddy?
MARGO: Be quiet, Narelle.

> *Pause.*

RUPERT: Do you know where he is?
JUNE: I'm his mother, I'm the last person you should ask.
MARGO: Probably staying with some bird.
RUPERT: He has a regular girlfriend?
MARGO: Yeah, or whoever was in the pub tonight.
RUPERT: You're sure he's not here?
NARELLE: He's not here.

RUPERT: He'll likely come back here at some point.
JUNE: If you say so.
RUPERT: Ask him to come down to the station. Or I'll be back.
JUNE: What's he done?
RUPERT: Just get him to do it.
JUNE: Or what?
RUPERT: What's been going on here tonight?
MARGO: A little ash, from a cigarette, caught the end of a mattress.
RUPERT: Can I come in and see?
JUNE: If you want to climb over my dead body.
MARGO: There's really no need.
NARELLE: Yeah, all the excitement is finished.

> JUNE *hugs* NARELLE.

JUNE: That's right, bubby, all the excitement is well and truly over with and it's time for you to go back to bed.
NARELLE: Do I have to?
RUPERT: Get the child back in bed. But ask Oliver to come in and see us as soon as possible.
JUNE: If we see him.
RUPERT: Thank you, Mrs Macreadie.
JUNE: Thank you, officer.

> RUPERT *exits.*

> MARGO *holds* NARELLE *and shakes her.*

MARGO: Where'd you learn to lie like that?
NARELLE: I just said what you said.
MARGO: Don't you dare try to lay the blame at my door.
JUNE: Margo!
MARGO: What?
JUNE: Leave the child alone.
MARGO: I'll do what I want, she's my kid.
JUNE: She was brilliant.
MARGO: Brilliant. She was a little liar. 'He's not here' and 'All the excitement's finished'.
JUNE: What would you rather they did? Search the bloody house like you gave them the chance to do by setting the bloody beds on fire.

ACT ONE 19

NARELLE: I can go and get him.
MARGO & JUNE: [*together*] Get back into bed.
>   NARELLE *looks at* JUNE.

MARGO: Don't look at your grandmother. I said, get back into bed.
JUNE: Go on now.
MARGO: She doesn't listen to a word I say.
JUNE: Shut up, Margo.
MARGO: Go on, tell me to shut up in front of her. Then she'll never listen to me.
JUNE: Haven't you done enough tonight?
MARGO: I haven't dragged the cops down on you, have I?
JUNE: I don't know what you think you're gonna sleep on.
MARGO: I'll sleep in with Narelle.
JUNE: Please yourself.
>   NARELLE *and* MARGO *get into the single bed. They turn over and go to sleep.*
>
>   OLLIE *enters.*

OLLIE: Have they gone?
JUNE: What's it about, Ollie?
OLLIE: I don't know.
JUNE: I told them you weren't here.
OLLIE: Thank you.
JUNE: You've done something.
OLLIE: I haven't.
JUNE: Did they see something in your car?
OLLIE: No.
JUNE: Did they plant something in your car?
OLLIE: No.
JUNE: Then what's in the back of your car?
OLLIE: Nothing.
JUNE: There was when I looked.
OLLIE: Why did you check my car?
JUNE: I don't trust you.
OLLIE: I thought you loved me.
JUNE: I do love you, but I don't trust you.

OLLIE: You can't love someone and not trust them.
JUNE: Don't be a drongo. Women all over the world love their husbands and don't trust them as far as they could throw them.
OLLIE: And does that include Dad?
JUNE: Dad wouldn't lie to me. He wouldn't dare. So don't you start.

   Pause.

OLLIE: I've been a mug.
JUNE: I know that for free.
OLLIE: This bloke in the pub asked if I'd like to move some stuff for him and said he'd give me a fifty.
JUNE: What stuff?
OLLIE: It's just a couple of those new pop-up toasters.

   Beat.

And some French perfume.

   Beat.

And a couple of crates of your Frigate.

   Beat.

Rum.

JUNE: Move it where?
OLLIE: That's just it. I took the stuff to the address he says and it's an empty lot in Darlinghurst.
JUNE: So you're left holding.
OLLIE: Yeah. If I keep the stuff it's receiving stolen goods, if I get caught with him it's called consorting.
JUNE: I know what it's called. Have you done this before?
OLLIE: …
JUNE: Cough it up, son.
OLLIE: It was easy money, Mum.
JUNE: There's no such thing.
OLLIE: I need to store it somewhere until I can get rid of it.
JUNE: You haven't heard from him?
OLLIE: No.
JUNE: Then that's why the cop came round. To let you know that they know you're left with it.
OLLIE: But if I can get it back to him before I go in to see the cops.

ACT ONE 21

JUNE *is getting really agitated now.*

JUNE: I think the bloke who gave it to you told the cops that you have it.

OLLIE: Why would he tell the cops?

JUNE: If he's a police informant, he gives them a little fish like you so they let him carry on with whatever he's doing.

OLLIE: No.

JUNE: Yes. Yes, Ollie. Any crim in this city, any cop in this town, they're two sides, one coin. How many other times?

OLLIE: Twice before.

JUNE: God help me. Are you the prize bloody fool of Pyrmont?

OLLIE: Mum?

JUNE: If you've done it more than once he's probably told them about that too.

OLLIE: Why would he?

JUNE: If you move this stuff or store this stuff it doesn't matter, he can tell them about those other jobs as well.

OLLIE: The fuckin' rat dobber.

JUNE: Did he give you a name?

OLLIE: Yeah.

Pause.

JUNE: Well?

OLLIE: Big guy. I dunno, Len, Ken.

JUNE*'s face changes, shocked.*

Mum?

JUNE: Wait.

OLLIE: What is it?

JUNE: Get away from me.

OLLIE: Mum.

JUNE: [*screaming*] Big guy, five eleven, name of Lennie McPherson.

JUNE *wails.*

SID *rushes onstage, just woken up.*

I'm telling you, Ollie. Stay clear of that snitch. Or one minute you're lying to me about cops at my door and the next minute the snitch is in Copper Kelly's ear.

SID: What's going on?

JUNE: Lennie McFuckingPherson. Lennie McDobberPherson has come after my son.
OLLIE: How does she know anything about this guy?
SID: Go to bed, now.
OLLIE: I just said I'd move some stuff for him. That's all.
JUNE: Police informant looking for someone to pin something on and you just volunteered with both feet.

    JUNE wails.

SID: Ollie. Go to bed. We'll sort it in the morning.
OLLIE: You don't know. You don't know that it's even the same bloke.
JUNE: As sure as there's cold shit in a dead cat.

    Pause.

SID: Will you go to bed, Oliver. Or God help me I'll shove you into it myself.
OLLIE: Well, what is she on about?

SCENE FIVE

SID *and* JUNE *are in bed.*

SID: You gonna be able to sleep?
JUNE: Fat chance.
SID: Then how about a bit?
JUNE: A bit of what?
SID: A bit of alright.
JUNE: Now?
SID: Come on, won't take a minute.
JUNE: And that's the bit I'm supposed to look forward to, is it?
SID: You do look forward to it, well you certainly did the last time …
JUNE: With my daughter having left her husband and my son having committed some crime I don't even really want to know about?
SID: So relieve the tension.
JUNE: You got stung today.
SID: What?
JUNE: I can always tell when you got stung because it makes you randy.
SID: Are you suggesting that there's something in a bee's stinger that works an effect on me?

ACT ONE 23

JUNE: It must be.
SID: So I need to carry them home in my clothes more often.
JUNE: You bloody better not.
SID: I've done it before.
JUNE: I know you did. That was me that got stung in that instance.
SID: Wanna get stung again?
JUNE: You'll be lucky.
SID: It doesn't hurt, except maybe a little at first.
JUNE: That detail is not going to sweeten me up.
SID: No?
JUNE: No.
SID: Which can only lead you to one conclusion?
JUNE: And what would that be, Mr Macreadie?
SID: That I like you all the better a little bitter.

He kisses her.

JUNE: What will we do if Lennie comes calling?
SID: I don't think it's the same Lennie. From what I've heard he's too busy taking down the SP bookie racket.
JUNE: But what if it is?
SID: If it is we'll sort it out.
JUNE: I thought I'd left it behind me.
SID: It's just the pain, just the fear.
JUNE: But why is it all still there, all still finding a voice in the confusion and dark?
SID: You've got to not let it get a hold of you.
JUNE: But it can all go wrong.
SID: It can but it might not.
JUNE: It grabbed hold of me, luv, like a tap turned on full, spewing out filth and bile and horror about what if and …
SID: Come on.
JUNE: … and the whole life, the whole crew, and the violence and the shame of it all.
SID: And that's when the fear gets bigger than anything else in your head.
JUNE: It's not just in my head. I'll put money on Lennie had something to do with Ryan getting pinched.
SID: Maybe.

JUNE: Soon as I saw it was Kelly who copper'd him.
SID: Growing it bigger in your head doesn't help anyone. He's just been a mug.
JUNE: If they find out he's a son of mine, he'll draw the short straw fast.
SID: He's got my name.
JUNE: Yeah, and my luck.
SID: Come on, my mo-lassy. You slap and I'll tickle.
JUNE: You tickle and I'll shoot through.
SID: No. Don't do that.

He kisses her again. She doesn't resist. They embrace.

SCENE SIX

The next morning.

The Macreadies' kitchen. MARGO *is making a cup of tea.*

MARGO: How did you sleep?
JUNE: I didn't.
MARGO: Did you ask him what it was about?
JUNE: …
MARGO: And you're going to let him go down to the cop shop? Better tell him about his pedigree before he does that.
JUNE: Or what? Or you will?
MARGO: I didn't say that.
JUNE: No. Because you don't know.
MARGO: Oh, I don't know anything, me.
JUNE: Especially not while you need a babysitter, you don't.
MARGO: Quiet now, pig-ignorant Polly.
JUNE: And what about you, Margo? Running out on your husband in the middle of the afternoon. What do you think he did for his dinner?
MARGO: I couldn't give a rat's arse what he did for his dinner.
JUNE: Exactly.
MARGO: Have you asked? Have you asked why I'm running out on him? Have you any interest in that?
JUNE: Couldn't give a rat's arse.
MARGO: Not like you can for your baby boy.
JUNE: Not this morning, Margo.

ACT ONE

MARGO: Why not this morning? When his true colours will be on display, if only you had the eyes to see them.
JUNE: Shut up or … God help me …
MARGO: God help you what?
JUNE: This is still my house.
MARGO: This is Dad's house. Because of Dad's job at CSR. And you don't own it any more than he does.
JUNE: And this morning it is likely to melt away with all my tears.
MARGO: Listen to yourself.
JUNE: Margo, for pity's sake. Stop it.
MARGO: Likely to melt away with all your tears! You never cried when I got pregnant. You never cried when I got married. You're not crying now that it's all going wrong.
JUNE: None of them things are likely to get you killed though, are they?
MARGO: What?
JUNE: You saw the news. You know that they're hanging Ronald Ryan.

Pause. MARGO *laughs.*

I will … God help me … I will throw you out of this house.
MARGO: You think that they're going to hang Ollie?
JUNE: Once he's in the system anything can happen.
MARGO: Mum!
JUNE: You tell me it can't happen and I'll call you a liar.
MARGO: They don't just hang people for nothing.
JUNE: They don't say it's nothing.
MARGO: Ronald Ryan killed a prison guard.
JUNE: There's some doubt about that.
MARGO: But Ollie is not even accused of killing someone.

Beat.

Is he?
JUNE: Don't even say it, Margo.
MARGO: They haven't hung anyone in NSW for years.
JUNE: But they can, Margo, they can. And they do it in my name.
MARGO: They haven't hung Ryan yet.
JUNE: But they will.
MARGO: But not Ollie. Not for nicking a television.
JUNE: Tell me this.

Beat.

Who do they do it for? Not for me. I don't want to kill Ronald Ryan. I'll let them lock him up for the rest of his life, I'll see justice done for that poor guard's family, if that's what they want. But I don't want them to slaughter the likes of Ronald Ryan. Because you can bet your sweet bippy that his mother is not living the high life somewhere. She's living on someone else's say-so, at someone else's beck and call. Just waiting for the bad blood to rise to the surface.

    MARGO *takes her cup of tea.*

MARGO: So tell Ollie how that crime boss shot your brother. You don't think he hasn't heard rumours.

JUNE: He's heard nothing. I've made sure of that.

MARGO: You think.

JUNE: It's the other side of the city. He knows nothing.

MARGO: Shot him in broad daylight and then dumped him at sea. Tell him and see if you can shock some sense into him the way you used it to try to shock sense into me.

JUNE: And look how miserably I failed at that.

MARGO: Well, how come I can know but not him?

JUNE: Because you already went and spoilt yourself.

    Pause.

MARGO: Spoilt myself?

JUNE: I didn't mean that.

MARGO: Of course you did.

    MARGO *looks at her and exits.*

NARELLE: [*singing*] Up to my neck in beach sand,
    Up to my eyes in sky,
    Up to my waist in water,
    This is the Sydney life.

JUNE: [*singing*] Up to their teeth in corruption,
    Up to their nuts in lies,
    Turn up their nose in pretention,
    That is the Sydney life.

SCENE SEVEN

NARELLE *is sitting, staring at* OLLIE *and* JENNY *on the fold-down couch.* JENNY *is sprawled, half-naked out of the bed, and* OLLIE *is nuzzled at her other breast.*

JUNE *enters with a cup of tea and a pretty dressing-gown in her hand.* JUNE *sees* NARELLE, *puts her finger to her lips and walks out again.*

JUNE: [*calling loudly off*] Narelle, where are you?

> NARELLE *gets up and exits.* JENNY *wakes up and pulls the sheet over her as* JUNE *enters.*

Good morning.

JENNY: Good morning.

> JENNY *clutches the sheet around her more determinedly.*

JUNE: You've worn that. Here.

> *She hands* JENNY *the dressing-gown and then turns her back as* JENNY *stands. She then turns back and gives* JENNY *the cup of tea.*

Piece of toast to go with that?

> JENNY, *surprised, leaves the sleeping* OLLIE *and follows* JUNE *into the kitchen.*

Sleep well?

JENNY: I did actually.

JUNE: They're quite comfortable those night-and-day divans.

JENNY: They are.

JUNE: Not that I'd know. I've slept in my own bed for twenty years.

JENNY: Right.

JUNE: But I'll bet you get to test them out fairly regularly.

> *Pause.*

I didn't mean that.

JENNY: It's alright.

JUNE: No, it would have been alright if I'd meant it.

JENNY: Really.

JUNE: There have been many occasions where I've meant it.

JENNY: I'm sure.

JUNE: Many occasions.

JENNY: I'm sure he's very … popular with the ladies.

JUNE: No. I didn't mean that either. Oh, dear. I can't seem to do this very well. It's so much harder when you're trying to be clear.

JENNY: Especially if you're more used to being a bitch.

Pause.

Now it's my turn to apologise.

JUNE: Well, we're both being misunderstood.

JENNY: I'm sure that's the case.

JUNE: So let me just say it straight out so that there can be no … interpretation … shall we say.

JENNY: Great.

JUNE: Are you intending to see my son again?

JENNY: Well, that rather depends on him.

JUNE: Nonsense.

JENNY: Well, of course it does.

JUNE: No, my dear. The correct answer is that it rather depends on me.

JENNY: Oh.

JUNE: We're speaking plainly.

JENNY: Yes. I see. At least I think I do.

JUNE: Are you interested in him as a prospect?

JENNY: A prospect?

JUNE: Yes.

JENNY: Um … well. I've only known him two weeks.

JUNE: Yes. But you like him.

JENNY: For this stage of things … you're not asking me if the sex is good?

JUNE: I am absolutely not asking you if the sex is good.

JENNY: Terrific. Though it is.

JUNE: I'm asking you because you seemed to be rather … amused by your little run-in with the law.

JENNY: Well, I did see the funny side of it last night.

JUNE: You're pretty. The cops like 'em pretty. And you were naked.

JENNY: I believe I may have been.

JUNE: They'll like remembering that too. Given a bit of luck they might write it all off as a bit of a bad joke and pick on some other mug.

JENNY: Who might?

ACT ONE

JUNE: The Pyrmont Branch of the NSW Police Force. So can you come down to the station with us today?

Pause.

JENNY: I can't make them drop a charge just by fluttering my eyelashes.

JUNE: No, you might need to wear a low-cut dress as well.

Pause.

JENNY: You don't have much respect for girls like me, do you, June?

Pause.

JUNE: I give you credit for the fine art of feminine wiles.

JENNY: Whatever I can do to help.

JUNE *nods and exits.*

SID *enters.*

SID: How are you, Julie? Alright?

JENNY: It's Jenny.

SID: Jenny.

JENNY: I've just had a very strange conversation with your wife.

SID: I'm rather surprised to hear you say you've had any conversation at all.

JENNY: Absolutely.

SID: She must want something.

JENNY: I think ... I mean, I can't tell ... but I think she may be more worried about what he's got himself into than I thought.

SID: Where did you grow up, Jenny?

JENNY: Just outside of Adelaide. I came over here with a fella.

SID: Where's he?

JENNY: [*shrugging*] Shot through.

SID: So you're looking to stick your claws in here?

JENNY: Stick my claws in?

SID: Isn't that what you girls do?

JENNY: Usually fending us off with a stick, are you?

SID: Good-looking boy like that? She routinely takes to them with a cricket bat.

JENNY: Yeah, well, she asked me to come down to the station so she's not worried about that. If I didn't know better I'd say she's working herself up into some sort of tizz about it.

SID: You grow up being poor, Jenny, and you soon learn it is exactly the same thing as being guilty. They don't need a reason to jail you, or beat you, mistreat you or break you. Being born with the smoke of the char house in your lungs and the daily dusting of coal on your skin, and the scream of industry in your blood and your ears, that's her ticket to terror, my girl. You know why people struggle to get out of this suburb, out of this poverty, Jenny? Being poor is not unhappy, having nothing is not the worst thing. The worst thing is that being poor is dangerous—knowing no-one and no-one knowing you.

> *Beat.*

So if you don't mind heading down the station and doing whatever my wife has asked you to do, well, let's just say you'll go up a peg in my esteem if you do, Adelaide girl.

> SID *exits.*
>
> *Lights up on where* OLLIE *is still sleeping.* JENNY *goes back to him and gets back into bed. She feels under the sheets and wakes him up.*

JENNY: Thought that might get your attention.
OLLIE: Yeah. What you gonna do with it now that you got it?
JENNY: Nothing.
OLLIE: Nothing? That's not much of an answer.
JENNY: And this is not much for privacy.
OLLIE: Come on, no-one will notice.

> JENNY *pulls away from him.*

Yeah. And what'dya want?
JENNY: Who says I want something?
OLLIE: You're the one pulling on that handle like it's a door knob to the future.

> *Pause.*

JENNY: I've been talking to your mother.

> OLLIE *pulls away from her.*

Thinks it might be a good idea for me to come down the station with you.
OLLIE: Yeah, well, if Mum thinks it's a good idea.

JENNY: You gonna tell me what's going on?

Pause.

OLLIE: I think they might have me on the hook.

JENNY: Well, we thought that last night, didn't we, and then you pulled out your lucky charm.

OLLIE: That what you are?

JENNY: Maybe. Still, I don't do things just because your mum says to.

Pause. OLLIE *kisses her.*

I don't think one will convince me.

OLLIE: One kiss?

JENNY: One reason. I need a few. Some of them wildly convincing.

OLLIE: It might be better than you've ever had before.

JENNY: Maybe.

OLLIE: It might be worse than you've ever had before, and then you'll be dark about missing out.

JENNY: Maybe.

OLLIE: It might be rough in a way that shocks you first off, but then you find strangely appealing.

JENNY: Go on.

OLLIE: It might be gentle in a way that riles you first off, but then you find surprisingly enjoyable.

JENNY: Right.

OLLIE: So. How are we doing?

JENNY: You're getting warmer. But I need the killer reason. I need the cracker, the most convincing reason to absolutely, totally do it.

Pause.

OLLIE: Well, that's easy.

JENNY: What?

OLLIE: It might be love.

JENNY: What kind of love?

OLLIE: Heart beating so fast that you worry, I mean, really worry that you've got some sort of bodgy ticker and you really might, I mean really might, have a heart attack.

JENNY: Seeing stars, seeing colours. Aching so that you're shaking your fingers and your feet to get rid of the pain.

OLLIE: So that you can't remember how to open a can of beer.
JENNY: Never.
OLLIE: So that you forget how to get out of bed.
JENNY: You can just roll out.
OLLIE: You forget how to do that.
JENNY: That's just silly.
OLLIE: And that's how you are. Crazy in love, jabbering like a baby, laughing at your shadow.
JENNY: Smiling like a stupid, smiling fool.
OLLIE: Woken every morning with obscene but sweet nothings in your ear.
JENNY: What kind of obscene but sweet nothings?

He whispers in her ear.

Well. Since you asked so nicely.

SCENE EIGHT

A police station.

OLLIE, JENNY *and* JUNE *are waiting.* CONSTABLE RUPERT *enters. He puts a set of keys down on the table.*

RUPERT: Can I help you?
JUNE: They asked us to wait here.
RUPERT: Who did?
JUNE: At the front.
RUPERT: The desk sergeant?
JUNE: Yes.
RUPERT: You'll find that things will go a lot more quickly if you refer to them by their correct name.
JUNE: Of course.
RUPERT: So the desk sergeant asked you to wait here?
JUNE: Yes.
OLLIE: You asked me to come down to the station.
RUPERT: Come to make work for us, have you?
OLLIE: Or we can piss off.
RUPERT: Are you handing yourself in too?
JENNY: Me? Of course not.

RUPERT: Who are you then?
JENNY: His girlfriend.

Pause.

RUPERT: We'd better lock him up and throw away the key then, hadn't we?
JUNE: He'd just as soon forget it.
RUPERT: No, I'll just go and check. What name?
OLLIE: Macreadie.

He exits. He leaves the keys on the table but no-one touches them.

JUNE: Let's go.
OLLIE: I thought you said to come down myself.
JUNE: Be buggered. Let them come looking for you.
OLLIE: Well, what do you want us to do, just leg it out of here?
JUNE: Yeah, come on.
PENNY: I think we should too.
OLLIE: Alright. Let's do it.

RUPERT *returns.*

RUPERT: Where are you going?
OLLIE: Outside to get some air.
RUPERT: I've heard that before.

Beat. He picks up the keys.

What are these?
JENNY: They're your keys, you left them there before.

Pause.

RUPERT: You think I'd just leave police keys lying around?
OLLIE: Well, you did.
JUNE: Ollie. Shut it.
RUPERT: That'd be very serious, that would, to leave a set of police keys where just anyone could take them. If someone had left them on this table that would be an act of gross negligence and that could also land their owner in a lot of trouble.
JUNE: Not if no-one knows about it.
RUPERT: No-one knows about a Macreadie wanted for questioning either, but that doesn't mean there isn't trouble here.

JUNE: How about we just put these back on the table where she found them and whoever left them there can just pick them up, no questions asked.
RUPERT: Wouldn't it be nice if things worked out like that.

Beat.

Let me understand what you're saying. You want me to ignore the fact that these keys were found in your possession.
JUNE: Can you do that?
RUPERT: I can do that. But let me put this to you as well. If you'd like to persuade me to ignore that you might also like to persuade me to ignore any file I might find on young Mr Macreadie here.
JENNY: I thought you said that there was no record?
RUPERT: Well, it's a bit like the keys really. They were found but you're suggesting they weren't. I can start a file on Mr Macreadie or I can make the whole thing go away.
JUNE: How much?
RUPERT: One large.
JENNY: A thousand dollars?
RUPERT: Something else you trade in?

Pause.

JUNE: I'll get it.
RUPERT: Then for now he's free to leave.

RUPERT *exits one way,* JENNY *and* OLLIE *go another.* JUNE *remains on stage.*

NARELLE: [*singing*] Up to my eyebrows in sunshine,
  Fill up my stomach with pies,
  Wattle and sweet frangipani,
  This is the Sydney life.
JUNE: [*singing*] Up to your kidneys in kickbacks,
  Up to your elbows in bile,
  Stripped in the name of progress,
  That is the Sydney life.

SCENE NINE

MARGO *and* NARELLE *enter.*

MARGO: How'd he go at the station?
JUNE: I'm not sure.
MARGO: Well, is he in or out?
JUNE: Out.
MARGO: So it went well.
JUNE: It may not last.
MARGO: Well, there's a newsflash.

> JUNE *looks at her.*
> *Pause.*

I went back home and spoke to Lindsay.
JUNE: About what?
MARGO: Well, there's the thing.
JUNE: What thing?
MARGO: The thing that made me wonder.
JUNE: Why are you talking to him?
MARGO: He wanted to see Narelle.
JUNE: Well, even if you separate he's going to want to see Narelle.
MARGO: I know.
JUNE: So?
MARGO: I asked what he was eating.
JUNE: I thought you couldn't give a rat's arse.
MARGO: That's what I thought too, and then it just came out of my mouth: 'Have you been eating okay?'
JUNE: Well, there can't have been a lot of conversation starters to choose from.
MARGO: But food?
JUNE: It's a common enough concern.
MARGO: But isn't it something that you ask, I mean, isn't that something you want to know if you care about someone?
JUNE: It could be.
MARGO: That's what I thought.
JUNE: Or it could just be something to say.

MARGO: I think I still care about him.
JUNE: You said he didn't love you.
NARELLE: Because he hits you.

> *Pause.*

JUNE: If he's hit you, he's worth nothing.
MARGO: I provoked him.
JUNE: And is that what you want to teach your daughter?
MARGO: Well, who's taught me?
JUNE: What?
MARGO: Who's taught me, that I'm worth less?
JUNE: Than who?

> *Pause.*

MARGO: Tell me you're not thinking about Ollie?

> JUNE *looks at her.*

JUNE: Do you know what jail is?
MARGO: It's not jail you're scared of.
JUNE: Go on then. I'll take Narelle.
MARGO: Ask Grandma to tell you about her family in Balmain.
JUNE: Shut up, Margo.
NARELLE: I already know. You were the last in a family of ten.
JUNE: That's right, Doll, I was.
MARGO: And all of her brothers were in trouble with the law.
JUNE: See, Mummy's making up fairytales now.
MARGO: And in this fairytale, Nanna runs away with her sugar man, and Nanna doesn't have anything to do with her family ever again. Only you can't run away from who you are in a town this small.
NARELLE: Do we have cousins?
JUNE: Go, if you're going.

> *Pause.*

MARGO: You forgive his mistakes because he's a boy.
JUNE: Do I?
MARGO: Of course you do.

> MARGO *kisses* NARELLE.

You be a good girl for Nanna.
NARELLE: When will you come back?

MARGO: Soon.
NARELLE: You just need some time together. To work it all out.
MARGO: That's right.
NARELLE: And then you'll come back and get me.
MARGO: That's right.

>MARGO *stands. Then leaves.*

NARELLE: Is that true?
JUNE: Of course. She'll be back in no time.
NARELLE: No, I mean about Uncle Ollie.
JUNE: What about him?
NARELLE: Do you love him better because he's a boy?
JUNE: Of course not.
NARELLE: Why does Mummy think that?
JUNE: For some reason it's easier for Mummy to think that she's making mistakes because I don't love her as much.
NARELLE: So why is she making mistakes?
JUNE: Because we all do.
NARELLE: You don't.
JUNE: Come on now, we've got things to do.
NARELLE: Like what?
JUNE: Bring your book.
NARELLE: To where?
JUNE: Promise me you'll sit quietly, Doll. Promise me.
NARELLE: I promise, Nanna.

>JUNE *looks at her and ruffles her hair.*

SCENE TEN

JUNE *and* NARELLE *are outside the local School of Arts.*

JUNE: Just sit here and wait for me.
NARELLE: Why?
JUNE: Don't ask me. Just do it.
NARELLE: But—
JUNE: Come on, please, for Nanna's sake.
NARELLE: But how long will you be?
JUNE: Probably not long at all.

NARELLE: Who do you have to talk to?
JUNE: I'm the one asking the questions. I'm the one who has to go in and see this man. I need some help.
NARELLE: And what will I do out here?

Pause.

JUNE: Alright, but if you come in you have to be quiet and sit tight.

NARELLE *nods.*

JUNE *goes into the building.* NARELLE *sits in the corner.*

BRIAN TUSKAN *enters.*

Thank you for seeing me, Mr Tuskan.
BRIAN: A pleasure, Mrs Macreadie, what can I do for you?
JUNE: Never thought I'd need to.
BRIAN: Well, you never know.
JUNE: All those days, standing outside the polling booths.
BRIAN: You've been very loyal.
JUNE: Handing out how-to-vote leaflets.
BRIAN: You know that I'm grateful.
JUNE: Lot of them look at you funny.
BRIAN: Is that right?
JUNE: And talk rough to you.
BRIAN: I'm sorry about that.
JUNE: 'Wouldn't trust him to give us lot a butcher's hook.' That sort of thing.
BRIAN: How unpleasant.
JUNE: And putting your face on a placard in my front yard. That got defaced one year.
BRIAN: I have my opponents.
JUNE: You do.

Beat.

But you also have your friends. Some of them in high places.
BRIAN: What's this about?
JUNE: My son's got himself into some trouble.
BRIAN: I see.
JUNE: So if I wanted to protect him I might need a friend. If I wanted to report something.

ACT ONE

BRIAN: Something?
JUNE: Someone. A copper.
BRIAN: A police officer?
JUNE: A bent copper.

Pause.

BRIAN: If you wanted to discuss this ... hypothetically.
JUNE: No. I'm telling you straight.
BRIAN: I suggest you don't tell me straight for the moment, June.
JUNE: But I can tell you who he is. A copper who demanded money from me.

Pause.

BRIAN: I suggest that you don't do that.
JUNE: But that's what I come here to do. It's taken all my courage as well.
BRIAN: What I can tell you, June, is that I am initiating action in this area. Right now, strategically I can't tell you what but I am planning to look into it.
JUNE: Look into what?
BRIAN: Well, in the first instance, procedures for making a complaint against a public servant. Technically I'm his employer so I don't even know if you can report it to me because that might be seen as conflict of interest.

He stands.

Thank you for bringing me your concern.
JUNE: Hang on. What am I going to do now?
BRIAN: I would urge you to reconcile yourself to the fact that these things happen to young men, in most cases they get through it.
JUNE: What?
BRIAN: I bid you good day, Mrs Macreadie.

Pause.

JUNE: He wants a thousand dollars, and I don't have it.
BRIAN: It's bigger than one boy, June, don't stir up a hornet's nest.

He exits.

SCENE ELEVEN

It is outdoors in the early morning. February, 1967.
Both JUNE *and* NARELLE *are in their dressing-gowns.*

JUNE: Now Nanna's got a job for you. You be a good girl for Nanna. I want you to go to all the houses in this street and I want you to collect all the newspapers on their front lawns.

NARELLE: Every single house on the whole of John Street?

JUNE: Every house that gets a rolled-up local paper.

NARELLE: But there are so many houses on this street.

JUNE: Oh, not for you, you're a big girl. Now come on, do it for Nanna.

NARELLE: But why?

JUNE: Don't ask why, just do it.

NARELLE: But why can't people read their newspapers?

JUNE: What did I just say? Don't ask why. Why is not the word. Why? Do it.

NARELLE: Okay, Nanna.

JUNE: Good girl. Now go on.

> NARELLE *begins to run around the stage, finding newspapers in various places.*
>
> SID *emerges.*

SID: What are you doing up before sparrows' fart?

JUNE: Something stupid. Something bloody stupid.

SID: And you've got the girl in it too.

JUNE: The local paper prints the court appearances.

> SID *watches* NARELLE *collecting the newspapers.*

SID: It doesn't say he's been convicted.

JUNE: I don't want the neighbours to all see his name there.

SID: It just says he's going to court today.

JUNE: What a day.

SID: Come on now, love.

JUNE: I don't want them to read about Ollie today.

SID: So you've got the girl stealing their local paper.

JUNE: Ohwww!

> *She blows it off.*

ACT ONE 41

It's not stealing.

SID: With that attitude I'm not surprised the boy went wrong.

JUNE: You what?

SID: I was joking. It's early.

JUNE: You think this is funny.

SID: No, luv, come on. Come inside.

JUNE: You think I did something to make him go wrong?

SID: Of course I don't.

JUNE: You just said so. You think it's the bad blood coming out, don't you?

> NARELLE *comes over with all the rolled-up papers in her arms.*

NARELLE: What should I do with them, Nanna?

> JUNE *looks at them and then puts her hand to her face. She is trying not to show how upset she is.*

SID: Do you know how to do papier-mâché?

NARELLE: Yeah, you soak the paper in water.

SID: You soak the paper in water. That's right.

NARELLE: But why did we have to get the paper so early?

SID: Because that makes the papier-mâché better.

NARELLE: No it doesn't.

SID: If you get papier-mâché with morning dew on it then the figures you make can turn into real fairies and fly away, like all your troubles.

> NARELLE *looks at him.*

NARELLE: That's not true.

SID: How do you know?

NARELLE: Well.

SID: Have you ever made papier-mâché that's been pre-soaked in morning dew?

NARELLE: No, but …

SID: No. But that's how much your grandmother loves you. She gets out of her lovely warm bed to get up and collect dew-drenched papier-mâché for her granddaughter. [*Whispering*] And even if it isn't true, isn't it lovely of Nanna to want to try it out for you, just in case?

> NARELLE *looks at him, still not sure. But then she goes over to* JUNE *and gives her a hug.*

NARELLE: Thank you, Nanna.

    JUNE hugs NARELLE, hard.

    SID looks at his watch.

SID: Two minutes.

NARELLE: What's happening?

JUNE: Be quiet.

SID: They're hanging a man in Victoria, Narelle. And all around the country, all over this country, people are keeping a minute's silence. Tram drivers, bus drivers, they're pulling off the road right now. On all the radio stations, silence. And at the end of that silence, Narelle, a man will have been put to death by the state. And it's going to happen right … now.

    They stand, silent. SID exits.

SCENE TWELVE

Later that day, on the street, outside the court. JENNY *enters, dressed in good clothes. She sits, looking dazed.* JUNE *enters, also in good clothes. She walks to the centre of the stage, removes her good shoes, then sits down next to* JENNY. NARELLE *stands a little behind them both, saying nothing.*

JENNY: He'll be out in three.

JUNE: Let's see.

JENNY: He could be out earlier, if he does that thing.

JUNE: Good behaviour?

JENNY: Yeah.

JUNE: Or he could be out in twenty-five if that's what they want.

JENNY: Who?

JUNE: The cops run informants who run the SP racket. That way they make money and they keep control. Anyone who stands up to them or calls out their informants gets shot. Nine millimetre bullets, sub-machine gun, no questions asked.

JENNY: And how does Ollie fit in?

JUNE: Ollie would have been just one of the tiny little fish they throw the cops to convince everyone else that they're keeping the streets clean. And once you're inside all the rules change.

ACT ONE

JENNY *looks at* JUNE*'s abandoned shoes.*

JENNY: Are your feet hurting?
JUNE: My feet, my legs, my calves, my arms, my shoulders. Turns out, he's the spring in my step.
JENNY: You did what you could. He knows that.
JUNE: Yeah, he knows now that when it comes to the crunch I can do sweet bugger-all.
JENNY: None of us can.

JUNE *looks at her, a long, measured assessment through her pain.*

JUNE: You're not a mother.

Beat.

Truth be told, you're not anything. What are you doing here?
JENNY: I'm here because I want to be. Where's Sid and Margo?
JUNE: Gone to see the sky pilot and find out which slammer they're going to put him in.
JENNY: The what?
JUNE: The sky pilot. What they call the chaplain.
JENNY: You know all about it.
JUNE: I grew up with it, Jenny. Grew up with it, ran away from it, and now I find that it's been hiding in my clothes or in my hair or in my shoes.

Beat.

Hiding, just waiting to come out.

JUNE *is rocking now, beginning to get really upset.*

JENNY: I know it's going to be bad.

JUNE *falls from the seat, forward, onto her knees.*

JUNE: My little boy.
JENNY: He'll be alright.
JUNE: My darling little boy.
JENNY: He's not a little boy, June. He'll look after himself.
JUNE: I couldn't help you. I'm useless. Useless. A useless, stupid, old woman.
JENNY: June!

NARELLE *goes over to* JUNE *and cuddles her.*

I want you to be part of the arrangements.
JUNE: What arrangements?
JENNY: Well, I suppose that sky pilot will have to do the ceremony.

> JUNE *looks at her, ashen.*

JUNE: The funeral?
JENNY: The wedding.
JUNE: Whose wedding?
JENNY: Mine and Ollie's.
JUNE: You're marrying him?
JENNY: Yes.
JUNE: Now?

> JENNY *nods.* JUNE *gets up and looks at her.*

How far along are you?
JENNY: I'm not pregnant.
JUNE: So why would you?
JENNY: I love him.

> *Pause.*

JUNE: [*pleased*] You're a bloody idiot.
JENNY: I guess I must be. Well?

SCENE THIRTEEN

At the Macreadie home.

JUNE, SID, JENNY, NARELLE, *and* MARGO *all assemble for a meal.* NARELLE *sets the table behind the others.*

SID: He's going to the Bay then?
JENNY: Yep.
JUNE: No beds. Tubs for their toilet. They put them out in the yard, exposed, for hours on end, in the rain in the cold. If they get sick there's bugger-all medical treatment. If they're not out in the cold they're in their cells for more than seventeen hours a day.
NARELLE: Are they going to hang Uncle Ollie?
SID: No, Doll, of course they're not.
JUNE: They hanged a man this morning.
SID: Yeah, and the sheriff broke down crying.

ACT ONE

JENNY: What sheriff?
SID: The sheriff who read the death warrant on Ryan.

Pause.

JUNE: The judge opposed it.
SID: Yes, but he still passed it.
JUNE: But he opposed it. All his life he opposed it.
MARGO: Ryan was manacled.
JUNE: Why are you saying that?
MARGO: I just … he was handcuffed, that's all.
JUNE: You shouldn't say that.
SID: June.
JUNE: Well, she shouldn't.
MARGO: Why shouldn't I say it?
JUNE: Because you're glorying in it.
MARGO: I'm not.
JENNY: She's not, June, come on.
JUNE: She's glorying in the little details.
MARGO: What about you, you're the one talking about the judge and the sheriff.
JUNE: Yes, but not about Ryan himself. Not about all the juicy details of what they did to him. Not all the ghoulish details of what they did to him.

Pause.

NARELLE: What would happen if the rope broke?
JUNE: See, that's what comes of it.
MARGO: She would have asked anyway.
JUNE: Not if you hadn't opened the door for it.
MARGO: So now you can tell me what I can and can't say to my own daughter.
JENNY: I don't think that's what your mother was saying.
MARGO: And you can shut it too. You and the stained-bloody-sheet brigade.
JUNE: Don't speak to her like that.
MARGO: Don't speak to her. What about me? You speak to me like that.
SID: Come on, Margo.
MARGO: And in front of my own daughter.

SID: They make sure that the rope is strong enough to hold the weight of the man they're going to hang, child.
NARELLE: And what if they get it wrong?
SID: It doesn't do anyone good to think about that, love.
JUNE: Grindlay stood with him.

>*Beat.*

He was his governor at Bendigo.

>*Beat.*

He said that Ryan was a model prisoner.

>*Beat.*

There's a campaign to get hanging abolished now. In every state.
SID: The Federal Parliament can still commit someone to death.
MARGO: Yeah, but why would they bother with someone like Ollie?

>*Pause.*

JUNE: I don't know what's made you like you are, Margo. Sometimes I think they must have swapped babies at the hospital.

>*Pause.* MARGO *sets her mouth and looks like she might cry but is biting it back.*

SID: That's a bit steep, love. Come on, both of you, nobody means what they're saying. It's a terrible day. A terrible day.
MARGO: Oh, she means it, alright.
JENNY: No, she doesn't.

>MARGO *gets up and leaves the table.*

Margo.

>JENNY *exits after her.*

SID: Go on.
JUNE: What?
SID: You've lost your son, do you want to lose your daughter as well? And with me on my bloody last legs.
NARELLE: What's Poppa talking about, Nanna?
JUNE: He's feeling miserable, that's all, like we all are.
NARELLE: Those bees haven't made him sick, have they?
JUNE: No, darling.

ACT ONE

NARELLE: Maybe it's just the fear in Nanna's head.

Pause.

SID: Little Miss Big Ears.

JUNE: How do you know about that?

NARELLE: I heard you talking with Poppa about it. What is it?

JUNE: It's nothing. It's just something Poppa helps me with.

He starts coughing.

And that's why he has to stick around, 'cause without him, those fears will get the better of me.

They all look at each other.

SID: [*with difficulty*] Narelle, come here.

NARELLE *goes to him.*

You know how sometimes you get really angry or really scared or really, really, really upset about something?

NARELLE *looks at him.*

When I first met Nanna she would sometimes talk to me about herself, about her life.

NARELLE: And some of it was sad.

SID: Yes. But I made Nanna laugh because I called that part of her—that part that is sort of her but more the scared, angry part of her—I call that her mo-lassy.

NARELLE: I know. Because when you make sugar the molasses are all dark and sticky and they're like sludge.

SID: Some people call it the black dog. But that's when you're sad. And Nanna's is not sad so much as …

NARELLE: … kind of burning, deep down. And when you said she was your mo-lassy that made Nanna laugh, didn't it?

SID: Yes, it did. And that's why she married me.

Beat.

Do you think you can make Nanna laugh about it?

JUNE: Sidney Macreadie. Don't lay that burden on this poor eight-year-old child. I can deal with my own demons.

NARELLE: You'll stop them from hanging Ollie, won't you, Nanna?

SID *is coughing again.*

JUNE: There is going to be a campaign. And there's gonna be lawyers and all that doing the bulk of it. But they'll be wanting shitkickers too, sending out letters and other things.

    SID *looks at her. He gets up from the table and goes after* MARGO.

    NARELLE *cuddles into* JUNE.

NARELLE: You'll stop them, Nanna.

JUNE: No, luv. But we'll make a bit of noise, shall we?

    She squeezes NARELLE *and kisses her on the head.*

NARELLE: No, you'll stop them hanging people, Nanna. You will.

    JUNE *shakes her head, squeezing her granddaughter again.*

Shall we put a bet on it?

JUNE: They'll be bloody long odds, my love.

NARELLE: Twenty-to-one?

JUNE: More.

NARELLE: Forty-to-one?

JUNE: I think more.

NARELLE: No bookie will go more than forty-to-one.

JUNE: Forty-to-one it is then.

NARELLE: By when?

JUNE: I can't do this, sweetheart.

NARELLE: Yes, you can. By when?

JUNE: A hundred years.

NARELLE: Ten years?

JUNE: No.

NARELLE: Ten years. Forty-to-one.

JUNE: Ten years.

NARELLE: I'll be nineteen. Just three years younger than Uncle Ollie is now.

    JUNE *is terribly upset.*

And what will it say, Nanna?

JUNE: It doesn't need to say much.

NARELLE: What?

JUNE: Just. That you can't kill no-one. But put better.

NARELLE: It's a bet.

ACT ONE

JUNE *looks at her.*

Nanna?
JUNE: Yes?
NARELLE: Is it the fear that gives you bad blood?

JUNE *turns her around and smacks her across the bottom.*

JUNE: I don't want to hear you ever say anything like that ever again.

NARELLE *looks at her with fury and runs off, crying.*

MARGO *and* SID *enter.*

MARGO: Come on, we're going home. Where's Narelle?
JUNE: You'll need to go after her.
MARGO: Go after her where?
JUNE: She just took off.
MARGO: Why?
JUNE: She can't have gone far.
MARGO: What have you done?
JUNE: I smacked her.
SID: You smacked her?
MARGO: I don't want you smacking my daughter.
JUNE: Well, I did. So you'd better go after her.
MARGO: So now you're taking it out on her?
JUNE: If the cops find her out wandering the streets they could charge you with neglect and take her from us.
SID: Come on now, luv.
JUNE: Because they can. They can. They can do anything to us that they want. They can make us criminals for the smallest thing while they get away with murder. They can talk about us diddling the system while they fiddle it like a violin. They can take my son and they can take my granddaughter.
SID: Where might she go?
JUNE: The swing set.
MARGO: The corner shops.

Pause.

ALL: The Sugar House.

SID, MARGO *and* JUNE *run off.*

SCENE FOURTEEN

The sound, the noise, the smells of machinery in the CSR factory.
NARELLE *is under a table, all scrunched up. She has her coat from 2007 on again.*
SID *and* JUNE *enter.*

SID: [*gently*] Here she is.
JUNE: Hello, Doll.
NARELLE: Hello, Nanna.
JUNE: We're very glad to see you, sweetheart.
NARELLE: Mmmm.
SID: What you doing here, luv?
NARELLE: Dunno.
JUNE: Your mum couldn't find you. She was worried.
NARELLE: Where is she?
JUNE: She's gone to look for you at the shops. Do you want to come out and we can go and meet her there?
NARELLE: Nah.
JUNE: You want to stay where you are?
NARELLE: Yep.

    SID *is having trouble breathing. He is coughing.*

What's wrong with Poppa?
SID: I'm alright, Doll, just had to run to get here.

    SID*'s breathing gets much worse.*

JUNE: Poppa's just going to go and sign on and tell them we're all here.
NARELLE: Why does he have to do that?
JUNE: It's a safety thing.
NARELLE: I'm safe.
JUNE: I know. But he still has to tell the foreman.
SID: That's right, squirt. I'll be back in a jiff.

    SID *exits.*

JUNE: I'm sorry I smacked you, Doll.
NARELLE: Why did you?
JUNE: I saw red. I'm sorry.

ACT ONE

NARELLE: You've never done that before.
JUNE: And I'll never do it again.

Pause.

NARELLE: Have I got dirty blood?
JUNE: No, you haven't.
NARELLE: Uncle Ollie has. So Mum must too.
JUNE: It's not just … it's not just your blood, sweetie.
NARELLE: What is it?
JUNE: It's what you make of yourself.
NARELLE: Then why'd you have to run away?
JUNE: I didn't run away. I just lost contact with the rest of my family.
NARELLE: How come?
JUNE: I just did.
NARELLE: So maybe I need to lose contact with all of you. Especially Uncle Ollie.
JUNE: No.
NARELLE: I am. I'm full of dirty blood.
JUNE: You're not.
NARELLE: I am. The kids at school all say I am.
JUNE: What people say doesn't matter two hoots.
NARELLE: It matters a lot. Otherwise we wouldn't have picked up all those newspapers.
JUNE: Come on, luv. Let's talk about this at home.
NARELLE: I'm not put together right.
JUNE: You think I believe that?
NARELLE: No, but you're just being nice.
JUNE: When am I nice? I'm cranky and scary and tough as all buggery. Isn't that what Mum says?
NARELLE: Yes.
JUNE: There has never been a child put together as perfectly as God put you together, for me.
NARELLE: That's not true.
JUNE: Yes it is. Because I happen to know that you have the original bee's knees.
NARELLE: I do not. They'd be too small.
JUNE: Will you come here to Nanna?

NARELLE crawls to JUNE.

Look at that hand.

They both look.

What do you see?
NARELLE: Just my fingers.
JUNE: Five perfect fingers. Now lift up those feet. What do you see?
NARELLE: Ten perfect toes.
JUNE: That's right.

Beat.

There is no such thing as bad blood, Narelle. There are bad laws and bad deeds, bad advice and bad decisions. But there is no bad blood. And you, Narelle, you are going to get educated and sophisticated and you are going to get up and out of here. Do you believe me?
NARELLE: Is that what you want, Nanna?

JUNE nods.

JUNE: Will you stay here a moment while I find Poppa and tell him we want fish and chips for dinner?

JUNE exits.

SCENE FIFTEEN

2007.

The lights change and NARELLE *is standing in the present, staring out at the lights of the city.*

A Jacksons Landing SECURITY GUARD *enters.*

GUARD: Do you use a different name every time you book in to be shown around?
NARELLE: No, I have to use my real name.
GUARD: And always different agents?
NARELLE: Well, it's such a big development they get listed with different agents all the time.

Beat.

The other guards won't come to this section, will they?
GUARD: No.

ACT ONE 53

NARELLE: I keep planning to go straight home.
GUARD: I wish you would.
NARELLE: I wish I would too.
GUARD: You can't sleep here again.
NARELLE: I won't.
GUARD: But you will.
NARELLE: I don't mean to.
GUARD: But you have. Three times. On the floor. In the time since…
NARELLE: You can say it. Since she died.
GUARD: You want me to sit with you?
NARELLE: No. You do your rounds. I may need to come down to the toilet later.
GUARD: If there's another guard down with me at some point …
NARELLE: I got lost looking for a guest.

Beat.

I know the script.
GUARD: You can't keep coming here.
NARELLE: I miss her. I miss them all. I miss what this suburb was.

Beat.

I think I miss what I was.
GUARD: What were you? A bony little punk full of too much attitude.
NARELLE: Yeah, a scrappy little insurgency shouting from the sidelines.
GUARD: I miss her too.
NARELLE: Let me stay.
GUARD: And then what?
NARELLE: And then I'll work out what I need to do.
GUARD: You're not going to work, you're not going home.
NARELLE: I'm trying. I'm trying to move on. I'm trying.
GUARD: Are you feeling unstable? A bit rocky road.

Pause.

NARELLE: I just need to be here. When I'm here it's clearer. I promise. I promise I'm going to get back on the horse. I promise I am.

They stand together for a moment.

He kisses her on the cheek.

GUARD: Text me if you want something to eat, Narelle.
NARELLE: Thanks, Uncle Ollie.

> *He exits. She drinks from a hip flask.*
> *The lights go out.*

END OF ACT ONE

ACT TWO

SCENE ONE

1985.

Police station.

A puked-up, drunken NARELLE *is sitting forlornly on a bench, her head down.*

RUPERT: Name.
NARELLE: Narelle Macreadie.
RUPERT: Address.
NARELLE: Harris Street, Ultimo.
RUPERT: Date.
NARELLE: 19th December, 1985.

SCENE TWO

1985.

Jenny and Ollie's home.

NARELLE: I did not assault a police officer.
JENNY: Please try to calm down.
NARELLE: But I didn't assault anyone. He assaulted me.
JENNY: They said you were resisting arrest.
NARELLE: Because I hadn't done anything.
JENNY: Why would you put yourself in a position where they can arrest you at all?
NARELLE: It was a peaceful demonstration.
JENNY: Let's talk about it later.
NARELLE: They were the ones who turned it violent.
JENNY: And why would you turn up to a protest when you're drunk and disorderly as well?

Pause.

NARELLE: Do you even know what disorderly is?
JENNY: Leave it, Narelle.

NARELLE: No, I'm just saying disorderly has to be more than just not orderly.
JENNY: What are you doing? You struggle to get into law school, you struggle to pay your way, you cook steak sandwiches for cab drivers and truckies at the late-night servo just to make ends meet, and then you get drunk and get arrested at a demonstration.
NARELLE: We had a few drinks before we got to the demo, that's all.
JENNY: It's not like you.
NARELLE: Thank you for coming to get me.

> *Beat.*

You won't tell Nanna.
JENNY: I won't tell Nanna.

> *Pause.*

NARELLE: Where is Uncle Ollie?
JENNY: He'll be home soon.
NARELLE: I should go.
JENNY: Narelle, tell me what's going on.
NARELLE: This girl I go to uni with? We met up at her place.
JENNY: And where does she live?
NARELLE: Dover Heights.
JENNY: Ah.
NARELLE: You should have seen this place. I walk in and it's at night, right. And there's this big, black area one side of the house and I say, is that the waterfront? And she says no and flicks on a light, 'That's the tennis courts'. And these people have got their own private tennis courts in their backyard. This girl, she talked about how hard she'd had to work to get into law school. And now I can say I've finally met one.
JENNY: Met one what?
NARELLE: A Liberal voter. I've never even met one before.

> OLLIE *enters behind a large, plastic Christmas tree in a box, which he proceeds to assemble and decorate.*

OLLIE: Look out, here's trouble.

> NARELLE *struggles to look sober.* JENNY *shakes her head at* OLLIE.

What's going on?

ACT TWO

NARELLE: Nothing.
JENNY: Just talking.

> *But this only makes him more suspicious.*

OLLIE: Come and give your old uncle a kiss hello, then.

> NARELLE *looks green, like she might be sick.* OLLIE *goes over to her to give her a kiss.*

Phwarr! Someone's been out on the turps? That's not like you, Doll.

> JENNY *looks pleadingly at* OLLIE.

NARELLE: What sort of tree did you have when you were a kid, Jenny?
JENNY: I dunno. It was green, it was pine. They're all much of a muchness.
NARELLE: No. You can get silver tinsel trees, you can get green plastic trees, like that one, or you can even get real ones.
JENNY: Yes.
NARELLE: You had a real tree?
JENNY: Sometimes.
NARELLE: Would you want to suggest that to Nanna?
JENNY: Real trees are horrible. You watch them slowly die in the corner, going a kind of yellowed brown, and then all the pine needles fall off.
NARELLE: But, it's more Christmassy.
OLLIE: Where did you see a real tree?
NARELLE: At this party I went to. This girl from uni.
OLLIE: You should invite her round.

> JENNY*'s eyes are pleading with* OLLIE *to drop it.*

I'll bet she's never seen a plastic Christmas tree before.

> NARELLE *looks at him wryly.*

You know, when Dad died and she had to move out of that house, one of the few things Nanna would have owned was this plastic Christmas tree.
NARELLE: I know.
OLLIE: You shouldn't be ashamed of that.
NARELLE: I'm not ashamed. I'm proud.
JENNY: You're defiantly proud. Which is the same thing as being secretly ashamed.
NARELLE: You're wrong. I just thought a real tree would be a nice change.

> OLLIE *is putting decorations on the tree.*

OLLIE: You're makin' friends at uni?
NARELLE: [*shrugging*] Not really.
OLLIE: Why not?
NARELLE: All they talk about is how to get things for free. Even though they've got heaps of money to pay for them.
JENNY: You must be makin' some friends if they're inviting you to their place.
NARELLE: I'm part of an action group.
OLLIE: A what?
NARELLE: It's just very small at the moment.
OLLIE: Yeah, and what's the action?
NARELLE: We're sort of still deciding that. We're anarchists.
JENNY: Do they have them now, do they?
NARELLE: What?
JENNY: Anarchist lawyers?
NARELLE: Do you even know what an anarchist is?
OLLIE: Anarchists believe in no centralised state and lawyers uphold the rule of law.
JENNY: And you can't be a lawyer if you get a police record.
NARELLE: I'm probably not going to become a lawyer.

> OLLIE *looks at* JENNY.

OLLIE: Spit it out. My eyes are itching from the wool you're trying to pull over them.
NARELLE: So I got arrested. They released me without charge.
JENNY: This time.

> OLLIE *launches at* NARELLE *and grabs her by the arms and shoves her up against the wall.*

OLLIE: Don't you fuckin' involve yourself in that.
JENNY: Ollie!
OLLIE: You ever do that again and I'll have your arse in a slingshot.
JENNY: Let go of her.
OLLIE: I mean it, Pup, I fuckin' mean it. Your nanna hears you got thrown in the back of a paddy wagon and it'll break her heart.
NARELLE: I have a right to public protest.
OLLIE: You have no right to do anything, anything at all that involves playing lock-up with cops. You stay out of that action group or God

ACT TWO

knows I'll bash you so hard you won't know if it's Christmas or Tuesday.

JENNY: Let go of her!

JENNY drags him off her.

What's got into you?

OLLIE: I'm not letting her become a fucking anarchist.

NARELLE: I'll go to demos, protests, actions, anything at all. If they do another women's camp protest at Pine Gap I'll be at the wire with all the rest.

OLLIE: I'm warning you.

NARELLE: I don't answer to you.

OLLIE: Oh, so now you're better than me. That what those rich cunts have taught you, is it?

JENNY: Ollie!

OLLIE: You listen to me, Narelle.

NARELLE: Why should I?

OLLIE: You listen to me or I'll knock you senseless.

NARELLE: You think I'm going to listen to some thug? Some barely-educated thug?

He launches at her again and they fight. He pins her by the neck. Then he pulls away. NARELLE *is crying and really fired up now.*

Deaths in custody is the same thing as deaths by hanging or electrocution or firing squad.

OLLIE: You think that?

NARELLE: This is what Nanna should be fighting against.

OLLIE: You think that?

NARELLE: Not some academic crap to take three obscure laws off the books. And I can do what I want. I can do whatever I want.

OLLIE: Why do you think I got an extra three years in jail from this lot?

NARELLE: What?

OLLIE: Why do you think I got three years more than my original sentence?

NARELLE: You were not prepared to salute a warder.

OLLIE: Face the wall. Hold your hands above your head. Fold your blankets this way, fold your toilet paper that way. All of those things I was prepared to do. I got three extra years because I was not prepared to salute a warder 'in recognition of the authority of the Sovereign'. I was not prepared to do that.

JENNY: You're a bloody idiot.

OLLIE: The lavatories are overflowing and open, and when you get out of the shower you step into the wetness of other prisoners' piss. I wasn't gonna salute a warder who'd house human beings like that, nor a Sovereign who would tolerate him doing so in her name.

NARELLE: And all I want to do is keep fighting for change.

OLLIE: Your Nanna has been fighting to quiet her own demons. And that's the beginning and end of it.

JENNY: Why do you say that?

OLLIE: Because they told me that they were targeting me. This is for being part of a family who stood up to Lennie McPherson who was a police informant and his detective mates.

Pause.

NARELLE: Have you told Nanna that?

OLLIE: Nanna knew that and she never told me. Because she was so ashamed she couldn't speak it aloud. But I'm telling you. If you go off on this demo, or whatever you're calling it, and you get arrested, don't expect you're going to get bailed like your little mates whose barrister daddy will make it all go away. And once you're in there, don't be surprised if they target you.

NARELLE: You're talking about a grudge from twenty years ago.

Beat.

How would any cop working today know anything about me?

OLLIE: It's written all over you, Pup. It's as plain as the eye can see that you're not one of them.

NARELLE: There were forty-eight deaths in custody last year. In 1984. Last year.

OLLIE: You're talking about Aborigines?

NARELLE: No, but of forty-eight deaths, six were Aborigines. And the legal profession are doing fuck-all. And they won't. Because they're part of the problem.

JENNY: So this is the same as your Nanna wanting the death penalty abolished?

NARELLE: This is more relevant than what she's doing now. She's just tidying up obscure laws that no-one even uses.

ACT TWO 61

OLLIE: Listen to you … takin' your life in your hands saying your Nanna's fight isn't relevant.
NARELLE: I wouldn't say it to her. But you've got to admit it's a bit fucking obscure. Caring about whether they change the legal details. So what if they can still hang some bastard in New South Wales for arson in naval dockyards, for Christ's sake. They don't need to wait to hang them. They killed forty-eight last year in prison or in custody. Forty-seven the year before, forty-two in '80 and '81. Forty people killed by the fucking cops every fucking year.
OLLIE: Oi. Since when do you get a mouth like a wharf labourer?
JENNY: It's not about what they can hang you for. It's the fact that they still can.
NARELLE: Yeah, but they wouldn't.
OLLIE: And if you say to your grandmother that her working for that big lawyer, Sheahan, is not a real fight, she'll be doing the cancan dance all bloody Christmas.
NARELLE: All she is doing is minding their kids while the lawyers talk to the politicians. Anyone can do that. She can wipe babies' bums anywhere and it's not going to change the world. She's not really doing anything. They're the ones dotting the i's and crossing the t's. And all for what boils down to a done deal.
OLLIE: Not a done deal to any bastard at the end of a rope for treason, piracy or arson.
NARELLE: In naval dockyards.
JENNY: And you know that your grandmother would say that Australia is still in bad company on the list of those countries who do still allow capital punishment at all.
NARELLE: I know.
JENNY: I said I wouldn't tell your grandmother about the arrest. But probably not going to finish your degree? I would have given my eye teeth to have the opportunities you're getting.
NARELLE: 'You should be grateful, Narelle.'
JENNY: Well, you should be. But you took one look at that tennis court and you thought, 'I'm never going to be able to make it anyway so why bother even trying'.
OLLIE: What tennis court?
JENNY: Never mind.

NARELLE: There are rich kids who know what I've been through. There are white-collar criminals. They just hide it better.

OLLIE: Well, that we can agree on.

Beat.

You remember that Christmas lunch when I was inside? Christmas decorations even. I think they had a Christmas tree in the entry hall. For the kids.

NARELLE: Yes.

OLLIE: That was organised by the wife of this crook accountant who was inside when I was there. She wanted to convince her kids that Dad was in a health facility for a couple of years.

NARELLE: The kids would have twigged.

OLLIE: I dunno. Some of those rich kids—if their brains were made of electricity they'd be a walking blackout.

NARELLE *smiles.*

Eh? Wouldn't know how to run a choko vine over an outdoor shithouse.

NARELLE *laughs.*

Listen, Pup. I'm sorry I scared you. But these kids you're running with … it's all a game to them. They want to play with the tough nuts who are bad fun. That is not you.

NARELLE: I want to do something.

OLLIE: Keep your head down and get your bit of paper.

NARELLE: And give up the action group. Just like that? Just because you say so.

OLLIE: Listen to me, Narelle, because I'm gonna say it once. You can run with this lot as long as you like. You can pass for as uppity as you like. But you're not one of them and you turn yourself inside out and you still won't be one of them.

NARELLE: You don't understand. And you don't want to. And I'm not giving up my politics because of some old scores that don't even matter anymore. It's 1985. The world's changed. And I'm gonna be part of that change. You all told Nanna to give it up. That she couldn't do it. And now you're telling me. Well, she wouldn't listen and neither will I.

ACT TWO 63

JENNY: Narelle.

NARELLE *exits.*

JENNY *shakes her head and exits.*

OLLIE *waits, then exits.*

SCENE THREE

The Office of the Attorney General, Goodsell Building, Chifley Square, Sydney.

JUNE: What are you doing here, Margo?
MARGO: Not today, Mum.
JUNE: What do you mean, not today? They said, 'Your daughter's downstairs to see you'. And I said, 'Be buggered she is, she doesn't know where I work'. And they said, 'She's downstairs in the foyer'. It gave me the fright of my life.
MARGO: Well, I might be able to top that in a moment.
JUNE: What are you thinking, visiting me in the city? What are you doing in town?
MARGO: I had to go to see a specialist near the town hall.
JUNE: What? What kind of specialist?
MARGO: Is there somewhere we can talk?
JUNE: You've never visited me in here. How'd you find it?
MARGO: I looked up Attorney General of NSW. You've climbed the ladder, haven't you?
JUNE: What? You think you need a title from the Queen to do babysitting?
MARGO: Wouldn't be surprised with this lot.
JUNE: They are having meetings today. And there'll be children for me to mind. I can't leave them in the room for long without getting back.
MARGO: There's a lump, Mum.
JUNE: What?
MARGO: They think it's spread to the lymph nodes.

Pause.

JUNE: Right.
MARGO: They're going to operate.
JUNE: When?
MARGO: As soon as possible. They take off the whole breast.

JUNE: Have you told Narelle?
MARGO: No. Will you?
JUNE: Why me?
MARGO: Don't play games, Mum, not now.
JUNE: How am I playing games?
MARGO: It will be better coming from you. She won't think the worst if it comes from you.
JUNE: Well, you shouldn't be thinking the worst either.
MARGO: But if it is the worst, you'll look after her. I'm not as sure as you about her going into the law. Living her life in places like this.
JUNE: It's what she wants.
MARGO: Yeah. But it's a recipe for a lifetime of carrying a chip on her shoulder.
JUNE: Well, you'd know about that.

Pause.

MARGO: Yep. I reckon I do.
JUNE: I didn't mean that.
MARGO: No. You never do.
JUNE: Come on. You'll beat this. You'll want to see her graduate, at least.
MARGO: I want to see her happy. This place, this lot. She's either gonna spend all her time sucking up to them or all her time spitting in their face. Either way she'll never just fit. One minute she's talking about making friends and loving it, the next she's sick of the lot of them and ready to chuck it in.
JUNE: Well, that's every young person.
MARGO: No, I didn't know what I wanted, but I knew where I was and who I was. Since she's been with this university mob, she's gone all spiky and resentful.
JUNE: It's the eighties, my love. Resentful is in vogue.

Pause.

That means it's common.
MARGO: I know what in vogue is, Mum.
JUNE: Narelle will be fine. And so will you.
MARGO: Seriously, I don't think she knows if she's Arthur or Martha at the moment.
JUNE: She's knows who the enemy is.

MARGO: Oh, yes, you've given her that. The fuel of resentment. The dartboard of blame. The great Australian struggle to put your problems down to someone else's persecution. I would have said she got that with her mother's milk, but really she got it from her grandmother.
JUNE: I won't apologise for teaching her to fight. She understands that this is a human rights struggle.
MARGO: In a way that I never have.
JUNE: Come on, let's not stand in a foyer and argue.
MARGO: But I never have. I hate your version of change. It's just all this sweat and blood and time that took you away from me. And her away from me. And you change it up and they change it back. And deep down, Mum, right deep down, I don't think it's the laws or the rope or even the suffering that motivates you. I think right deep down there's this scream inside you that just makes you want to lash out at the world and this one—this injustice, this absolute challenge to life and hope—it drives you because within it there is no possibility of redemption. And you need that hope, you need to believe in redemption more than anything. What scares you most? Most of all? That your granddaughter's newfound middle-class life will just be a thin topsoil over her ugly, ignorant, bad-blood past. A thin layer of advantage that can be blown away by the winds of change.

And that's why, in the luckiest country in the world, we crouch in fear, in terror of what our kids might, if we don't watch them, slip back to. It's what makes you and all the rest of us so ruthless and so mean. And what are you looking for, Mum? The day when people coming here will think we were never hungry, never poor, never wading through shit and choking on smoke, dying of rickets and whooping cough. You know the worst thing about pretending to be all polished and posh, people start to believe that's all you've ever been. They tear everything down in this city, tear it down, gussy it up. We paid for this city like everyone else, so why are we never listened to? Why are our memories and our sense of belonging so worthless in this city?
JUNE: Come here.

    JUNE *holds her arms open.*

MARGO: What are you doing?
JUNE: I'm giving you a hug.

MARGO: Since when?
JUNE: Since I learned it from those upper-class toffs upstairs. I've seen them give each other a hug when things are tough.
MARGO: And what good does that do?
JUNE: I dunno. But let's give it a waltz round the block, shall we?

> JUNE *goes to* MARGO *and hugs her.* MARGO *hugs her mother tightly, then exits.*

SCENE FOUR

The lights come up on TERENCE SHEAHAN. JUNE *goes over to him.*

JUNE: Mr Sheahan. Have you got a moment for that word I wanted to have with you?

> *Pause.*

SHEAHAN: Could we do it tomorrow, Mrs Macreadie?
JUNE: Absolutely.
SHEAHAN: I promise we'll get to it tomorrow.
JUNE: Of course. You're an important man.
SHEAHAN: If you say so.
JUNE: Exactly. And I do.
SHEAHAN: Well, that's very gratifying.
JUNE: A man unused to having to ask favours of anyone.
SHEAHAN: You'd be surprised.
JUNE: Normally I wouldn't even think about taking up your time.
SHEAHAN: Tomorrow for sure.
JUNE: I guess you're wondering what could be so important for the babysitter to interrupt you and demand time when this bill, this is so important. Don't I know it. You're gonna change the law. The last reasons they can kill people in NSW and therefore the last in Australia.
SHEAHAN: We're going to do it. And you've been a great help.
JUNE: And it was your father who introduced legislation in this state which outlawed the sentence of death for murder in 1955.
SHEAHAN: That's exactly right. Now if you will excuse me …
JUNE: And now, thirty years later, you're gonna introduce laws removing the last three crimes they can top you for.
SHEAHAN: Yes.

ACT TWO 67

JUNE: You and your family, you really do want to right the wrongs done for capital crimes.
SHEAHAN: Certainly.
JUNE: I've believed for many years that the most important way to bring that about is by changing the law. That's why I learnt to type. Did you know that?
SHEAHAN: No.
JUNE: I learned to type up articles. And your lot, the lawyers, they did focus groups about it, and what could I do? I could mind the kids while they filled in their forms and got their statistics.
SHEAHAN: Yes. Now, Mrs Macreadie, if you don't mind …
JUNE: I'll fight till my last breath is out of my body. I'll scream it until my last drop of blood leaks out of my veins. They have no right to take the life of our kids, poor kids, black or white, they're the same when they're poor. Black neck, white neck, snaps the same when you string it up.
SHEAHAN: Mrs Macreadie, I don't want to be rude, but I really do have to get on with my work. So perhaps you could just tell me what it is that you want?
JUNE: Mr Sheahan, will you give my granddaughter an opportunity to intern with you in the Attorney General's office?

>*Pause.*

She's twenty-six years old and just finishing her law degree. She knows all about you and your work, I know that she will work hard. I'm a canny woman, I'll tell you that, but when it comes to talking to you lot, I don't know the rules. I don't know the game, and frankly last time I asked a politician for something he threw me out and my son went to jail anyway. In my world, you do people a favour and they do you one. You scratch my back and I'll scratch yours. But that's not how it works with you lot, is it? It's a bloody tricky business, and see, I haven't got that kind of time.
SHEAHAN: Oh?
JUNE: Her mother has cancer. Her breast.
SHEAHAN: She's dying?

>*Pause.*

And why should I favour your granddaughter above others?

JUNE: Just because ya can. Because you're the one with all the power, not me.

Pause.

SHEAHAN: Make an appointment for her with my associate.
JUNE: Thank you.
SHEAHAN: I won't promise.
JUNE: I'll send her.

Beat.

Thank you.
SHEAHAN: Thank you, Mrs Macreadie.

JUNE hands him a Tupperware container with lamingtons.

What's this?
JUNE: It's lamingtons.
SHEAHAN: Could they be considered an inducement?
JUNE: Nah.
SHEAHAN: Well, they could.
JUNE: Trust me, I'm a lousy cook.

He shakes her hand. They exit in opposite directions.

SCENE FIVE

NARELLE *is in a tattoo parlour. She is lying on her back with her bottom exposed as the tattoo artist,* ZEE, *works.*

ZEE: Someone call you that?
NARELLE: What?
ZEE: Sugar?
NARELLE: No.

Beat.

It's a long story.
ZEE: We're gonna be here a while.
NARELLE: For three little sugar cubes?
ZEE: You want them to look like sugar cubes or blank dice?
NARELLE: Sugar cubes.
ZEE: Your mother calls you that?

ACT TWO 69

NARELLE: No, she called me Doll.
ZEE: But you didn't ask me for a rag dollie.
NARELLE: No.
ZEE: I'm doing a good job.
NARELLE: Good.
ZEE: But people still might think they're dice.
NARELLE: What people?
ZEE: People who see them.
NARELLE: Well, no-one is going to see them who I can't tell that they're sugar cubes.
ZEE: Right.
NARELLE: Right.

Pause.

ARTIST: So why does your mother call you Doll?
ZEE: I don't want to talk about my mother.
ARTIST: Doesn't like you?
ZEE: It's complicated. She's never been happy.
ARTIST: Face like a mile of unpaved road.

Pause.

ZEE: Yeah. Elegantly put.
ARTIST: Hey. I'm a visual person.

ZEE continues working.

NARELLE: Is it always a symbol for something? I mean, the people who come in.
ZEE: Why do you do that?
NARELLE: What?
ZEE: Play dumb.
NARELLE: I'm not.
ZEE: Is it always a symbol for something when people come in to get a permanent body tattoo? Well, derr. Of course it's always a symbol. Luvvie. You know that. And you know what yours is a symbol for, but for some reason you don't want to tell me, which is cool, you know. Totally cool.

Pause.

NARELLE: Can you stop?

ZEE: Seriously.

NARELLE: Yes. Stop please.

ZEE: You don't want me to leave it like that.

NARELLE: Well, I don't want to be heavied while I've got my bum exposed to someone I don't know who is lecturing me about playing dumb.

Pause. ZEE *turns off the ink needle and* NARELLE *sits up.*

ZEE: You alright?

NARELLE: It's … Just give me a minute.

ZEE: Hey. Hey. This happens all the time. Seriously. It's a deal being inked. A deal. And sometimes it helps to talk about what's happening and sometimes it doesn't. And if I got it wrong, I'm sorry, babe.

Pause.

NARELLE: Okay.

ZEE: Yeah?

NARELLE: Yeah.

ZEE: You want me to keep going?

NARELLE: I just maybe need to take five.

Pause. ZEE *sits down and cleans another needle.*

ZEE: You got weekend plans?

NARELLE: Why do you want to know?

ZEE: Sister, you gotta relax, girl. I'm just making conversation.

Pause.

NARELLE: Matter of fact I do have plans this weekend.

ZEE: Yeah?

NARELLE: Turns out I'm going to a demo.

ZEE: Good for you.

NARELLE: Deaths in jail. When they hold people in custody, you know.

ZEE: Right.

NARELLE: Sometimes they beat people to death. String them up and make it look like suicide.

ZEE: You gonna amp up about that, girl? Go for it.

NARELLE: Yeah. I think I will.

ZEE: You *think* you will or you will?

NARELLE: I will.

ACT TWO 71

ZEE: You have to learn to hold your nerve.
NARELLE: I can do that.
ZEE: Not so's I've seen.

> *Pause.*

NARELLE: You do a good line in free abuse.
ZEE: I was at an antinuclear rally. And a bloke I'd known for years he saw the cops coming. Took one look and ran. And he sort of explained himself later but, you know, it was never the same. With the others, he was blanked so dead, blanked right off the scale. Labelled a coward. Savage it was. Just so you know.

> *The* ARTIST *exits.*

SCENE SIX

NARELLE *stands as* JUNE *enters.*

JUNE: Let me have a look at it.
NARELLE: No, I just want to put something on it to stop the stinging.
JUNE: Should have gone to outpatients.
NARELLE: Not for a tattoo.
JUNE: Then let me look at it.

> *She looks at the tattoo.*
>
> Interesting position.

NARELLE: Does it look infected?
JUNE: Is it supposed to be a candelabra?
NARELLE: No.
JUNE: A caterpillar?
NARELLE: No.

> *Pause.*

JUNE: Never mind. It will only be seen when you're being fucked from behind.
NARELLE: What … are you doing?
JUNE: Well, now that you've got a tattoo, I thought … I mean … That's how women talk, you know, in jail.
NARELLE: I should never have come.
JUNE: Me or septicaemia, huh?

NARELLE: This, if you're wondering, is why I don't visit so often anymore.
JUNE: Really? Let's just have a listen to my answering machine messages. Have to work. Have to study. Have to work and study. Have to drink. Have to work, study, drink and get a tattoo. Have to find my brain which I lost the day I got a tattoo.
NARELLE: Yeah? Well, you've well and truly opened the door now. Grandma.
JUNE: Have I? Opened the door? To what?
NARELLE: Vulgarity. That was the most vulgar thing to say to me, to me, that you just said.
JUNE: Well, I'd say you opened the door to vulgarity with your little skin picture, cupcake.
NARELLE: There was this voice saying, 'Don't go to see her. She'll nag you, she'll lecture you, she'll try to control you like she's always done.'
JUNE: Is that what I've always done? I thought what I've always done is help you and encourage you.
NARELLE: To be you. You encourage me to be a version of you.
JUNE: What?
NARELLE: Nothing.
JUNE: You know what?
NARELLE: I'm right?
JUNE: Well, I was going to say you should get a hepatitis shot, but by all means say you're right again if you need to.
NARELLE: I'd rather fucking drink my own urine and shit standing up than ever come round here again.
JUNE: That thing stays infected and you may be doing just that.
NARELLE: And good. Because I'd actually rather die than have to get a degree that I don't want, and go to work in a profession that I hate just because you want me to. Yes, that's right. I'm chucking it in. I'm withdrawing my place. I'm not going to finish my law degree.
JUNE: Just to piss me off.
NARELLE: No, Nanna, not to piss you or anyone off. Because I don't want to. Because it's not me.
JUNE: Do you know how many generations it's taken for you to be able to go to university?

ACT TWO

NARELLE: Here we go.

JUNE: No, really, do you know what it has cost? The actual price. Not in dollars.

NARELLE: I don't want to listen to this.

She begins to leave.

JUNE: You've heard of razor gangs? Well, that was my brothers. They cut people with razors. Slashed their faces, their necks. And they did it because where we lived, there was no electricity. Only a fuel stove. And me in my nightdress at the front door, telling the cops that my brothers weren't home.

Beat.

My father coming home with no skin on his back because he'd been loading raw soda ash down on the wharves. And that's why my brothers didn't want to work, they wanted to get their money some easier way, and if that meant challenging the crime boss of the day, they did. And one of them came off the worse for wear. Dead. Dumped at sea. And the whole family in the shit up to their eyeballs. You come round here and you wave your privilege at me as if it's something that you were just born having. I have paid for that university degree with my guts and my days. Can you see that? Can you just for a moment pull your head up out of your selfish little tattooed backside and recognise what we have done for you?

NARELLE: No, Nanna. I can't. Because what you want for me is a dream, a fantasy, an idea of what I should want, not what I do really want.

JUNE: And what's that?

NARELLE: I don't know. And that's actually okay. It's okay not to know until you do. It's not a crime to be unsure.

JUNE: Not a crime. But it's a luxury. A luxury I never had.

NARELLE: Yes, I know that. I know that better than I know just about anything.

JUNE: Then respect it.

NARELLE: I don't actually know what that means, Nanna. Respect it? By becoming a fake?

Pause.

JUNE: Well, when do you think you will know what you want to do?

NARELLE: Don't ask me that.
JUNE: I was trying to be understanding.
NARELLE: I don't know. I don't know what and I don't know when.
JUNE: Well, in the meantime could you try it my way?
NARELLE: No, because you have to not do the thing you don't want to to discover the thing you do.
JUNE: That sounds … I'm sorry, Doll, but that sounds ridiculous.
NARELLE: To you.
JUNE: To me who has wanted this for you for so long that there have been days when you were the only certain thing in my life.
NARELLE: Don't say that, Nanna.
JUNE: And if I think you're going to throw it all away, it's like being in a room where all the windows have been closed and there's no air and I try to breathe but it's just hot air, stale hot air that someone else has breathed before, air thick with molasses and smoke and I open my mouth to breathe and there's nothing, nothing, nothing.

She stops, her mouth open, trying to breathe.

Because, Narelle, my love for you is the only thing that lets me breathe. The only thing. If you said, 'I want to do this instead', or 'Will you help me go this way?', I could understand that. But 'I don't know'. 'I don't know'. What do I do with I don't know?
NARELLE: You wait. Like I have to wait.

Pause.

JUNE: I'm not going to let you throw your life away on 'don't knows'.
NARELLE: You can't do anything to change my mind about this, Nanna.
JUNE: You're going to pick up that phone and call Justice Sheahan and ask for an appointment.
NARELLE: No. I won't.
JUNE: And ask for the appointment he has already agreed to give you.
NARELLE: You asked him to help me?
JUNE: And why shouldn't I?
NARELLE: I can't believe this.
JUNE: Believe what?
NARELLE: This is so humiliating. Tell me you didn't take him in some, I dunno, some cake in a Tupperware container.
JUNE: Lamingtons.

ACT TWO

NARELLE: What?

JUNE: I took him some lamingtons. He thought they were very nice.

NARELLE: So he could look down on the funny little working-class lady still making her own lamingtons and asking favours for her little granddaughter.

JUNE: He's not like that.

NARELLE: They're all like that.

JUNE: This has been a very interesting talk, Narelle. I've let you say your piece, and I've listened, and now it's over.

NARELLE: Well, I still won't call him.

JUNE: Yes. You will.

NARELLE: I won't. Because it's wrong.

JUNE: You will do this. For me, for your mother and for your own future, which you don't even understand yet.

NARELLE: I won't call him. I won't do it. Because even if they let me in the door they'll never be fighting for the same things I am.

> JUNE *picks up a butter knife from the table and stabs it into the back of her own hand.* NARELLE *looks at her and the knife, sticking out of her grandmother, and turns white with shock.*

JUNE: Oh God, I'm sorry, Doll.

NARELLE: Nanna, what are you doing? Why did you do that?

JUNE: I'm sorry.

NARELLE: Don't pull it out.

JUNE: It's not bleeding.

NARELLE: I'll go … and call … I'll … what will I do?

JUNE: Get me a bandage. It'll be alright. I missed the tendons.

NARELLE: Why did you do that?

JUNE: I'm sorry.

> *Pause.*

NARELLE: Have you done that before?

> JUNE *puts her other hand to her mouth, rocking back and forth with the horror of what she's done.* NARELLE *wraps something around her hand.*

JUNE: Your mother is sick, Narelle.

NARELLE: What?

JUNE: She's been having tests.
NARELLE: Why didn't you tell me?
JUNE: How? By calling around to all the tattoo parlours in Sydney?
NARELLE: Can you drop it?
JUNE: Like you dropped your pants?
NARELLE: Nanna.
JUNE: We'll talk about it on the way.
NARELLE: Where?
JUNE: To the hospital. Unless you want to wait and see if my hand is going to fall off.

They exit.

SCENE SEVEN

JENNY, *who is wearing a pink cleaner's uniform, is screwing nuts onto bolts and then throwing them into a box.* OLLIE *emerges, scratching his head as if he has just woken up.*

JENNY: Hello, luv.
OLLIE: I was gonna get up and do them.
JENNY: You needed to sleep. What time did you get back?
OLLIE: About half past three.
JENNY: Good run?
OLLIE: Yeah, straight through to Melbourne and straight back.
JENNY: Truck alright?
OLLIE: Yeah. Leave those, I'll finish them.
JENNY: No need, I'm done. The boss wants them by tonight.
OLLIE: I'll do the bulk of the next batch.
JENNY: Ollie, they're just a little side earner. Get some more sleep if you need it.
OLLIE: Mike reckons I'm mad not to do the No-Doz pills to stay awake.
JENNY: Screw your system with that shit.
OLLIE: Don't I know it.
JENNY: Then again, you don't want to fall asleep at the wheel.
OLLIE: I'm not gonna fall asleep. I've got too much to live for.

He grabs her to him and gives her an affectionate kiss. JENNY *starts unbuttoning her blouse.*

ACT TWO

JENNY: You do want me to keep going?
OLLIE: Of course.

> JENNY *continues unbuttoning her blouse, finally taking it off altogether. She begins to unzip* OLLIE*'s fly.*

Wait.
JENNY: What?
OLLIE: Just … nothing.
JENNY: We don't have to.

> OLLIE *says nothing.* JENNY *puts her shirt on and begins to button it up.*

Do I look older? Is that it?
OLLIE: You look gorgeous.
JENNY: I look older.

> *Pause.*

OLLIE: I don't stand up and dance so much anymore, luv.

> *Pause.*

JENNY: We can do other things.
OLLIE: What other things?
JENNY: Your mouth still seems to be working alright.
OLLIE: Yeah? 1985 and the sexual revolution comes calling, eh?
JENNY: 'Bout time.
OLLIE: You're on.

> *He kisses her again.*

JENNY: I thought I'd go and visit Margo later.
OLLIE: Yeah.
JENNY: You want to come with me?

> *Pause.*

OLLIE: What's she doing in that hospital?
JENNY: Calvary.
OLLIE: Doesn't sound like the kinda place you get out of.
JENNY: It isn't. June reckons that everyone around her is … old … and …
OLLIE: Dying.
JENNY: Yep.
OLLIE: So what is she doing there?

JENNY: It's where your mum said she wanted to go. At the end.
OLLIE: I reckon that ups me.
JENNY: What?
OLLIE: Well. I thought going to jail took the cake. But dying before the old girl. I'm not gonna beat that.
JENNY: Ollie!
OLLIE: Fought all these years for all those mangy bastards not to die, so the fella upstairs takes her husband and now her daughter.

Pause.

And Margo's never stopped wanting June's approval. She acts like she doesn't need it, she gets meaner and ruder and makes out that she wouldn't want it even if it was there. But it eats away at her. Inside.
JENNY: Like cancer.
OLLIE: Like cancer.

Pause.

JENNY: You don't let it eat away at you.
OLLIE: Too bloody selfish for that. No, I'll be alright. Always some soft-hearted dame to pick up after me. Been livin' like that since I was in nappies, eh? Why stop now? No, I'll be fine. It's my sister that I can't …
JENNY: Save.

Pause.

OLLIE: She doesn't want to see me.
JENNY: Come with me and wait.
OLLIE: What good will that do?
JENNY: I'll tell her you're there for her. It's something.

JENNY exits.

SCENE EIGHT

NARELLE: [*singing*] Go tell the mountain to jump in the sea,
    To the sting of death, oh, say that you're free,
    Teach the high and mighty how to behave,
    Announce your victory o'er the grave.

Outside the hospital. OLLIE *enters and sits down.*

ACT TWO

Hi, Uncle Ollie.
OLLIE: Hi, Doll.
NARELLE: You going up?
OLLIE: Yeah. Just cooling my heels for a moment.
NARELLE: But you've been up to see her?
OLLIE: I will.
NARELLE: You should go up and give your sister a hard time.
OLLIE: I know.
NARELLE: You'll regret it if you don't.
OLLIE: I know. I'm hopeless about this stuff.
NARELLE: Yeah, you are.
OLLIE: Oi.
NARELLE: So we can both go in and be hopeless together.
OLLIE: Yeah. I will.
NARELLE: Or not.
OLLIE: Sorry, Doll.
NARELLE: Why have you always been the golden-haired boy and no matter what Mum does she can't turn a trick with Nanna?
OLLIE: [*shrugging*] Dunno. Why, have you?
NARELLE: Not anymore.

> *Pause.*

OLLIE: You gonna listen to me on that business with staying away from the cops and not getting involved with those troublemakers?
NARELLE: You going to pin me up on the wall again if I say no?
OLLIE: You watch me.

> *Pause.*

NARELLE: I won't get arrested.
OLLIE: You can't take the chance. You get a record and you'll never jump the bar.
NARELLE: You mean pass the bar.
OLLIE: That either.

> *Pause.*

NARELLE: I don't know what I'm going to do.
OLLIE: Go up and see your mother. Your protesting days can wait.

> OLLIE *exits.*

SCENE NINE

A hospital ward.

MARGO *is in bed, with a morphine drip.* JENNY *sits by her side as she sleeps.* JUNE *is also there, with a bandage on her hand.*

NARELLE *watches, without making her presence known.*

JUNE: Jenny is here, Margo.

MARGO: Jenny who?

> *Pause.*
>
> *A* DOCTOR *enters.*

JUNE: And now here's someone you'll really want to see.

> MARGO *opens her eyes and sits up.*

MARGO: Oh. It's you.

DOCTOR: Good morning.

MARGO: Thank you for coming, Lindsay.

DOCTOR: I'm sorry?

MARGO: I really didn't expect you'd come. How about that, Mum? Lindsay turned up after all. After all these years of making me wonder if I was ever married to him in the first place.

DOCTOR: [*to* JUNE] Who's Lindsay?

JUNE: Her ex-husband.

MARGO: I must look terrible. You might have given a girl some notice.

DOCTOR: Mrs Howe, it's me, Dr Stewart.

MARGO: I so wanted to see you … before. I've always loved you, you know.

JUNE: Margo.

MARGO: Have you seen Narelle? She's grown up that clever. You wouldn't believe it. Not with the two twits she had for parents. I mean, I don't mean you, though we both made mistakes really. But here you are. Come to clear the air, and after all these years.

JUNE: Margo, Lindsay's got to go now, so that you can see the doctor.

MARGO: Don't make him go yet, Mum. We've got to talk. We've got to catch up.

JUNE: He'll come back. You just have to see the doctor now.

ACT TWO

MARGO: Alright. Alright, Mum. Can you believe he came?
JUNE: I know. I know, luv. He must have really loved you.
MARGO: Yeah.

> JUNE *indicates to the* DOCTOR *to leave. Then suddenly* MARGO *grabs him.*

A kiss goodbye.

> *The* DOCTOR *looks at* JUNE *who glares at him. He leans in and kisses her, then exits.*
>
> MARGO *looks at him as he goes and turns to* JUNE.

That wasn't really him.
JUNE: …
MARGO: When he leaned in, I realised. Why did you do that, Mum?
JUNE: Because he doesn't love you enough to be here, but I do.
MARGO: I know you do.
JUNE: Do you?
MARGO: In your grumpy, crabby bitch of a way.
JUNE: In my grumpy, crabby bitch of a way I love you.
MARGO: We didn't play it very well.
JUNE: No, we really didn't.
MARGO: Why are you saying all this?
JUNE: Can't a mother tell her daughter she loves her?
MARGO: I'm really gonna die, aren't I, Mum?
JUNE: Yes, luv. You really are.
MARGO: I'm sorry. I'm so sorry.
JUNE: Come on. We conned a kiss out of that doctor, though.
MARGO: We did.
JUNE: He's too slow to keep worms in a tin.
MARGO: He is.
JUNE: What'dya reckon, Jenny? How far you think we can get him to go, eh?

> JENNY *laughs,* MARGO *laughs.*

MARGO: Big pash on the mouth, I reckon.
JUNE: Yeah. An' the rest!
JENNY: Mum!
JUNE: Listen to 'er with the 'Mum'.

MARGO: The woman we met wearing a sheet wrapped around her.
JENNY: That was years ago.

They all laugh.

It was either a striptease or a dirty great fine.

JUNE: An' she's still trying it in front of those new speed cameras they've introduced. Off with the gear, but the cameras aren't budging.

JENNY: I do not!

They all laugh.

NARELLE goes to her mother's bedside. MARGO *nods at* JUNE.

JUNE: Just in time to give us a break. Let's go get a cuppa, Jen.

They exit.

MARGO: Narelle.
NARELLE: Mum.
MARGO: What?
NARELLE: You know I like to be called Nell now.
MARGO: Soon you won't. Soon you'll want the name I've given you. That's all you'll need to remind you of me every day of your life.

Pause.

I was going to call you Gayle.

NARELLE: Gayle? I'm glad you called me Narelle.
MARGO: So I did one thing right.

Beat.

Will you do something for me?

NARELLE: Of course.
MARGO: Call this Sheahan character and tell him you would like to work for him.
NARELLE: I don't need him to do me any special favours.
MARGO: Of course you do. And you'll do it too. Get off your high horse and go and get yourself that job.
NARELLE: Is there anything you like about me, Mum?
MARGO: Sure. But you've got your Nanna to tell you how wonderful you are.
NARELLE: Not lately.
MARGO: Your uncle then.

ACT TWO

NARELLE: You know this is emotional blackmail?
MARGO: Yes, and you know you're going to have to stop being a self-absorbed little shit for a moment.
NARELLE: [*shocked*] I'm not.
MARGO: You are. This is a one-year job placement. I'm not asking you to give him a blow job.
NARELLE: Well, it feels like a betrayal of what I believe in.
MARGO: Only because at the moment you're a little up yourself, miss. If you don't do it, in ten years you'll feel like you betrayed my dying wish.
NARELLE: How can you say that to me? When you know I'll never forget what you say now?
MARGO: This is more important than anything I say. This is more important than me.
NARELLE: That's not true.
MARGO: Stop blubbering. It is true. You got love from your Nanna. You never needed it from me.

Pause.

Go call him.

NARELLE *nods.*

SCENE TEN

NARELLE *enters Sheahan's office. She is agitated, uncomfortable, not sure how to begin.*

SHEAHAN: Miss Macreadie, come in.

Beat.

You've taken your mother's maiden name.
NARELLE: My grandmother's name.
SHEAHAN: Yes.
NARELLE: She encouraged me to study law.
SHEAHAN: And how do you get on with your colleagues in the legal profession?
NARELLE: I have different values. They don't know much about what it's like to actually go hungry.
SHEAHAN: Probably think it's about the same as dieting.

NARELLE: I get all dressed up to hide what I don't have. While they are all trawling the op shops to hide what they do.
SHEAHAN: Downwardly mobile.
NARELLE: Is that what they call it?
SHEAHAN: You have a different perspective. That's valuable.
NARELLE: I see goodies and baddies. I see justice and grotesque injustice. I have a raging fury that sees everyone as with you or against you. That sees in black and white.
SHEAHAN: Then you might need to be fitted with glasses.
NARELLE: Four years of law school. Legal precedent. Case studies. Rhetoric. Argument. Logic. And now I'm not sure if I want to learn your way of seeing.
SHEAHAN: You're suspicious. And you're unbelievably arrogant. And maybe you're even stupid enough to blow an opportunity like this.
NARELLE: Have you offered the job to someone else?
SHEAHAN: I was promised a street-smart kid who works out how it all plays and beats me at my own game. Where's she?

 NARELLE *is so enraged that, for a moment, she can't speak. She paces.*

NARELLE: If I come to work here, will you announce an enquiry into prisoner deaths?
SHEAHAN: I won't do it just because you tell me to.
NARELLE: So you're just going to ignore what's going on?
SHEAHAN: I want to hear your perspective. I might not agree with you but I'm going to listen to you. And you're going to watch and learn how other people offer their perspective. You're going to watch and learn how to strategise to get what you want and get your voice to be heard. Right now you're a bull in a china shop, but I can teach you how to tiptoe through the tulips.

 NARELLE *stares at him.*

NARELLE: There's evidence that police are complicit in prisoner deaths during arrest and deaths in prisons.
SHEAHAN: In what states?
NARELLE: In all states.
SHEAHAN: And what is being done at the moment?
NARELLE: There's an enquiry which the NSW Attorney General's Office, your office, has been asked to make a submission to.

SHEAHAN: Is that a project you would like to undertake if you were to be attached to this office as an associate?
NARELLE: It is.
SHEAHAN: Alright then.

Pause.

NARELLE: Why would you do this?
SHEAHAN: I like your grandmother.
NARELLE: Liking someone only takes it so far with you people.
SHEAHAN: That's true. First you like someone, then they have to prove that they deserve the chance you can give them.
NARELLE: So how do you decide?
SHEAHAN: You believe in something other than yourself. That always has been and always will be surprisingly rare.
NARELLE: I'm not my sweet little grandmother, you know.
SHEAHAN: No. But she's not really that sweet when you get to know her either.
NARELLE: That's true.

Pause.

SHEAHAN: You'll start Monday?
NARELLE: Guess my protesting days are over.
SHEAHAN: You fight inside the system and you create real change. Or you can stand outside and scream. It really depends if you want the slow, compromising work of actual change, or the glamour of being a spoiler.

SHEAHAN *exits.*

SCENE ELEVEN

NARELLE *crosses the stage to where* MARGO *is in bed covered in a sheet.* JUNE *is holding her hand.* NARELLE *goes over to* JUNE.

NARELLE: Mum?

JUNE *gets up.*

JUNE: She died, honey.

Pause.

NARELLE: I wanted to tell her that I loved her.

JUNE: She knew.
NARELLE: I wanted to say it.
JUNE: She knew.

> *Pause.* NARELLE *pulls the sheet aside to kiss* MARGO *goodbye. There is a long silence.*

NARELLE: Sheahan asked me to be his intern.
JUNE: Good.
NARELLE: Mum made me call him.
JUNE: Sneaky.
NARELLE: Yeah.
JUNE: Played her last hand pretty well, then.
NARELLE: I'll say.

> *Beat.*

JUNE: I'm going to ask the nurse if she'll let me wash your mum's body.

> *She takes a bowl and begins to wash* MARGO, *using towels to conceal her body parts.*
>
> NARELLE *walks to the bathroom of the apartment and with a detachable shower nozzle wets only her head as she cries.*

ALL: [*except* MARGO, *singing*] Go tell the mountain to jump in the sea,
    To the sting of death, oh, say that you're free,
    Teach the high and mighty how to behave,
    Announce your victory o'er the grave.

    Walk on the water, but never drown,
    Fly over deserts yet to be found,
    Work all your life but no money save,
    For yours is a victory o'er the grave.

    Know who to trust and still who to doubt,
    The furnace consumes but hope is without,
    Give all your love with never a wave,
    Complete is your triumph o'er the grave.

    Some will go fast with a sigh of relief,
    Others do linger and paddle in grief,
    Women may babble and men they may rave
    Against the terror approaching the grave.

All of us end with a page to our name,
Read through the tears of a weeping refrain,
Our faults or our virtues will neither us save,
For none win a victory o'er the grave.

SCENE TWELVE

2007.

When she enters, PRIN *sees* NARELLE.

PRIN: I knew you would be.
NARELLE: I'm still here.
PRIN: I knew you would be. When you said you'd just get the umbrella. I should never have trusted you.

    OLLIE *enters.*

Now I really will have to ask you to leave.
OLLIE: It's alright.
PRIN: Why didn't you check this last night?
OLLIE: Keep your hair on, darling.
PRIN: You can't speak to me like that.
OLLIE: I know. But then I just opened my mouth and out it came. So bully for me.
NARELLE: Ollie.
PRIN: Do you two know each other?
NARELLE: [*simultaneous*] No.
OLLIE: [*simultaneous*] Yes.
PRIN: I'm going to have to report you for this.
NARELLE: No, listen, he let me stay because I'm going to buy it.
PRIN: You are?
NARELLE: I think so.
PRIN: You think so or you are?
OLLIE: You don't have to buy it just to let me keep my job.
NARELLE: No, I've decided. I have. I want to buy it.

    Pause. PRIN *looks from one to the other.*

PRIN: You'll need to come in and make a deposit for me to hold it.
NARELLE: I will.

    Pause.

PRIN: You need to look at the appropriate language protocols in the staff handbook.
OLLIE: Yeah, and you need to go soak your head in a bucket full of blue-green algae.
PRIN: Oh, you are so losing your job over this.
NARELLE: No he's not, because you were the one who let me go back for the umbrella. Legally you are the one responsible for my trespassing, and if you report him I will testify that the fault, the breach, was actually your negligence.

Pause.

PRIN: Are you a lawyer?
NARELLE: Yes. I am.
OLLIE: Go the legal eagle.
NARELLE: Thank you.

Pause.

OLLIE: How 'bout we just leave well enough alone.
PRIN: What does that mean?
NARELLE: It's like how 'bout we chill out and move on.
PRIN: Oh, right.
NARELLE: [*to* PRIN] My grandfather used to work here.
OLLIE: My father.
PRIN: At the sugar refinery?
NARELLE: Yes, and he used to bring me here, from when I was about eight.

PRIN *folds her arms.*

And his wife, my grandmother, died recently.
PRIN: Your mother?
NARELLE: My grandmother. June.
OLLIE: Come on.
NARELLE: I'm trying to explain to Pin.
PRIN: Prin.
NARELLE: Prin.
OLLIE: Short for Princess?
PRIN: Better than short for pin head.

They all laugh.

So your grandfather worked here?

ACT TWO

OLLIE: Yeah. He was a fitter and turner.
PRIN: So some of those machines preserved around the site he would have worked on?
OLLIE: They're the ones. Why?
PRIN: I get so many questions about them, you wouldn't believe. I mean, historical redevelopment, right, so people expect you to know what every piece of rusting old metal was used for. And I don't know.
OLLIE: Well, you only have to ask.
PRIN: Really?
OLLIE: Yeah.
PRIN: So would you walk round with me and just give me some little bits of stuff.
OLLIE: Stuff? Like facts?
PRIN: Yeah, that'd be great.
OLLIE: You get a commission on every sale?
PRIN: What?
OLLIE: Nah, I'm pulling your leg.
PRIN: Huh?
OLLIE: Thick as two short planks.
PRIN: Can we do that now? I've got four inspections today and the older clients really go for that historical line. Lots of them remember this place from their own childhoods. You'd be surprised how many of the residents who can afford a place like this now actually come from, you know …
NARELLE: Poverty.
PRIN: Yeah. That.

They begin to leave.

You'll come in if you decide to buy it.
NARELLE: Just one more look around and then I really will leave.

OLLIE winks at NARELLE as they exit.

NARELLE, in 2007, goes and sits under the trolley on which JUNE is washing MARGO's body.

JUNE: [*gently*] Here she is. Hello, Doll.
NARELLE: Hello, Nanna.
JUNE: I'm very glad to see you, sweetheart.
NARELLE: Mmmm.

JUNE: I thought you had a big criminal case.
NARELLE: Yeah. But …
JUNE: But what? I'm that proud of you. A partner in a bloody law firm. Who would have thought? Couple more years and they might even make you a judge.
NARELLE: No.
JUNE: What's wrong?
NARELLE: The barrister I'm working with wants to blame my client's crime on his bad blood. Only now they're calling it his DNA.
JUNE: That old chestnut?

They exchange a glance.

NARELLE: But there is no such thing as rust in the gene pool, is there, Nanna?
JUNE: You already knew that. What do you still need from me, Doll?

Pause.

NARELLE: Why did you want me to get up and out, Nanna? What did I get up and out of when I left you and this place behind?
JUNE: Because I wanted you to have choices, you twit.
NARELLE: You think I had a choice? Mum was unhappy and Dad was absent and Poppa was sick and Ollie was in trouble. But you were there. Root rock solid. Hard as marble and tough as nails. You kept your promises and you told me I would succeed.
JUNE: I believed in you.
NARELLE: You were strict and you were full of expectations.
JUNE: I said I'm proud of you, Narelle.
NARELLE: Because I have always done what I've been told to do by you.

Pause.

JUNE: Well, I'm sorry if I wanted you to do well.
NARELLE: I never stood up to you because I was scared of you.
JUNE: No, you weren't.
NARELLE: I *talked* a lot about rebellion. But I never did it.
JUNE: I saved you from throwing your life away.
NARELLE: You were strong and you were clear. You were like this suburb, June, like Pyrmont, tough and real and resilient. But when you didn't understand something or someone you'd crush them. And when I don't understand something fragile or delicate or subtle in myself I try to crush it. And that's what you did to Mum. And I watched what

ACT TWO

you did to her and I never wanted you to do it to me. I love that you made me tough, Nanna. I love being your nuggetty little battler. But to make me, you had to break Mum.

Pause. An uncomfortable silence.

JUNE *goes to* NARELLE.

JUNE: Look at that hand. What do you see?
NARELLE: Just my fingers.
JUNE: Five perfect fingers. Now lift up those feet. What do you see?
NARELLE: Ten perfect toes.

Pause.

JUNE: You're my legacy, Narelle. My flesh and blood, my faults and fears. I made you out of the soot and grit, out of the stones and joy and hope that I could find lying around.
NARELLE: I know. But where I am now …
JUNE: If it's suffocating you, you need to go find the mob who will let you scream your brains out. The sludge, the grief, the pain, the fight, that's who you are. They skim off those molasses when they make sugar, Doll, but those molasses … turns out they're the best bit.
NARELLE: But if you don't deceive your bees …
JUNE & NARELLE: … your bees will not deceive you.

[*Singing*] Fly away—die away—
Dwindle down and leave you!
But if you don't deceive your bees,
Your bees will not deceive you.

Don't you wait where the trees are,
When the lightning's at play,
Nor don't you hate where bees are,
Or else they'll pine away.

Pine away—dwine away—
Anything to leave you!
But if you never grieve your bees,
Your bees'll never grieve you.

Lights fade.

THE END

Belvoir presents

THE SUGAR HOUSE

By **ALANA VALENTINE**
Director **SARAH GOODES**

This production of The Sugar House *opened at Belvoir St Theatre on Wednesday 9 May 2018.*

Set Designer **MICHAEL HANKIN**
Costume Designer **EMMA VINE**
Lighting Designer **DAMIEN COOPER**
Composer **STEVE FRANCIS**
Sound Designer **MICHAEL TOISUTA**
Stage Manager **ISABELLA KERDIJK**
Assistant Stage Manager **KEIREN SMITH**
Stage Management Secondment
ELLA GRIFFIN

With
SHERIDAN HARBRIDGE
SACHA HORLER
LEX MARINOS
JOSH McCONVILLE
KRIS McQUADE
NIKKI SHIELS

The Sugar House *is supported by The Group.*

We acknowledge the Gadigal people of the Eora nation who are the traditional custodians of the land on which Belvoir St Theatre is built. We also pay respect to the Elders past and present, and all Aboriginal and Torres Strait Islander peoples.

PHOTOGRAPHY Daniel Boud
DESIGN Alphabet Studio

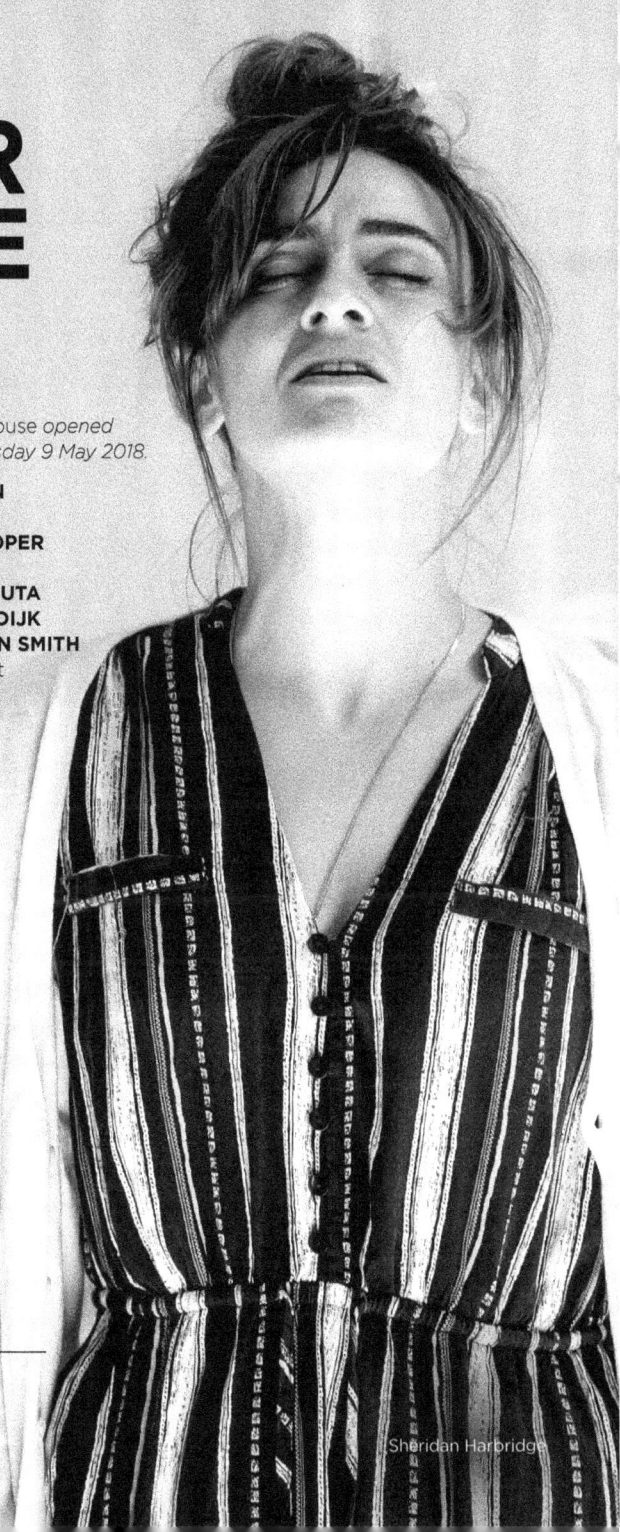

Sheridan Harbridge

WRITER'S NOTE

Alana Valentine

"Nostalgia is not always a soothing experience. It can produce rage at things unnecessarily destroyed and pain from a sense of irretrievable loss."

Frank Moorhouse, *Dupain's Australians*

In February this year I was invited to speak to the Pyrmont History Group. They hold their meetings in the former CSR Pay Office in Pyrmont, across Refinery Square, and next to the refurbished Cooperage which supplied the former CSR Distillery. I was told that the group brings together 'survivors of urban renewal and newcomers to the high-rise apartments that have replaced the cottages and the industrial buildings of CSR'. I suggested that we might read an excerpt of my work-in-progress play with local community members and, thankfully, several readers volunteered. One was a former judge, another a former teacher, and many were residents of the Jacksons Landing community. Jennice Kersh, a long-time Pyrmont local, had brought with her a volunteer called Barry, who had been a rabble-rousing union organiser. There was something about the authenticity of the place and the interaction of the readers which transformed the small community gathering into something very precious to me.

In much of my work as a dramatist, I strive to privilege voices which are drawn from diverse communities of interest. I do this because I believe in the value of connection and the piquancy of verity. I want to find freshness in the supposedly familiar and work with artistry with my theatre colleagues to bring that to audiences. In *The Sugar House* I have also drawn deeply on my own life and memories as a resource for the drama.

Although Pyrmont is a real site for the many conflicts between change and progress that play out in this and other cities, Pyrmont is also the ultimate metaphor for the unsolvable tensions inherent in both an individual and a community. The tensions between the value of the past, the needs of the present and the contract with the future. This fabulous Sydney suburb, which in 1992 declared itself the Republic of Pyrmont and issued passports to non-residents, is a potent dramatic frame for the obligations and decisions which we as individuals and citizens have to make every day. What to keep. What to discard.

When in 2017 *The Sugar House* was given an in-house reading by Belvoir, Eamon Flack described how, later, everyone in the office began to speak about their own families, about what had been facilitated to get them to their present reality. It is an enduring gift that he had the confidence to believe that the play might induce those same discussions in the Belvoir audience: to talk to each other about the 'not always soothing experience' of nostalgia as a provocation for how we decide the relative importance of respect for history and opportunities for change; to commune with characters who struggle to be equal to their ancestors' ambitions and want to understand how they came to be who they are; whose identity is deeply linked to their past even when it changes in the present; and, who need to reach into that past to resolve unspoken and uncomfortable truths.

I thank Neil Armfield for commissioning this play, and those who have offered dramaturgical advice, including Sam Strong, Anthea Williams and Wesley Enoch. I acclaim Sebastian Born, the former Associate Director (Literary) of the National Theatre, London, for his endorsement of this play. It was written for Kris McQuade and I cherish the honour of having such a legend on stage in my work, Sheridan Harbridge is my deepest idea of Narelle,

Sacha Horler's vitality and courage is a sincere inspiration, Josh McConville who is as dangerous and beautiful as my own Uncle Ross, to whom this play is lovingly dedicated, Nikki Shiels whose talent is astonishing, and Lex Marinos, a respected elder of our profession who brings his calm, clear magic to this ensemble.

When Sarah Goodes came with me into the Mitchell Library to look at original Max Dupain negatives, commissioned by CSR in the 50s and 60s, and which I had requested be thawed out from cold storage, I knew that her commitment to and passion for this work would transform it in remarkable, urgent ways. My thanks to the genius of her team, Michael Hankin, Damien Cooper, Emma Vine, Michael Toisuta and Isabella Kerdijk, and the cleverness of the Belvoir production staff including the departing Sally Withnell who will be much missed. To Steve Francis, whose work as a musical collaborator I continue to treasure. And I pay special tribute to Shirley Fitzgerald and Tim Peach, Mitchell librarian Helen Benacek, my agents Sharne McGee and Wendy Howell, Vicki Gordon, and Justice Terence Sheahan, former NSW Attorney General, whom I interviewed about the passage of his legislation in 1985 which finally abolished all capital punishment in Australia.

Alana Valentine
Photograph by Patrick Boland

DIRECTOR'S NOTE

Sarah Goodes

When I first read Alana's play I was struck by the family drama at the heart of it: the often tragic triangle of tension that lies within families – two people who don't know how to love each other and one person stuck in the middle.

However at the same time, it's a play about Sydney – Australia's biggest and fastest changing city. This beautiful play examines Sydney's past through the Macreadie Family, exploring the city's criminal history and the idea of inherited shame. It skates between the personal and political in a way I haven't experienced in a new work for a while. I wanted to tell this story with a focus on sunlight and actors in a nearly empty space. The main design springboard was the photography of Max Dupain and Olive Cotton and their shared fascination with Sydney's dazzling light and deep shadows. I knew lighting designer Damien Cooper would have a field day creating these moods in this space he knows so well. So too for designer Michael Hankin whose familiarity with and knowledge of the Belvoir building enabled him to conceive a design that celebrates the factory origins of the theatre while allowing the magic realism of a memory play to emerge. Costume designer Emma Vine has meticulously researched the era and unearthed gems and costumes from magical places. Composer Steve Francis and I talked a lot about the kind of music we needed to evoke the famous dancing Sydney light. He has written beautiful pieces to Alana's lyrics, and Michael Toisuta's soundscapes weave it all together.

Of course the core of this work is the writing and the actors who bring it to life. They are a rare and insanely talented group of performers who have been a joy to work with.

I spent a lot of time looking at the Belvoir anniversary book and loved actor and writer Rita Kaljenais' essay about the incredible grace and bravery actors bring with them on to stage, night after night:

"Theatre should always be about connection and revelation. An actor's job is to connect with the audience, with other actors, with a greater truth. When I sit in a dark theatre and someone on stage reveals the truth of their heart to me and I feel my own beat in response, I feel grace. When I stand on stage connecting with an audience whose presence makes a story bigger than me, it's there."

Something in Alana's play feels bigger than us all – it amplifies the complexities of families' inheritance, shame, love, and living in a city as big, beautiful and, at times, ruthless as Sydney.

We hope you enjoy being with it as much as we have enjoyed bringing it to life.

Sarah Goodes

BIOGRAPHIES

ALANA VALENTINE Writer

Alana's previous works for Belvoir are *Barbara and the Camp Dogs* (co-written with Ursula Yovich), *Parramatta Girls* and *Run Rabbit Run*. *Ladies Day* at Griffin in 2016 was nominated for the Nick Enright Prize for Drama, NSW Premier's Literary Awards. She received two 2017 Errol Awards for *The Tree Widows* and was nominated for Best Director for that work. In 2018 Alana is working with Bangarra Dance Theatre as dramaturg on *Dark Emu* after previously working with Stephen Page on *Bennelong*, *Patyegarang* and *ID*. In 2018 Merrigong Theatre Company will tour *Letters to Lindy* to 20 venues in NSW, Victoria, Queensland, and the Northern Territory including Darwin and Alice Springs. In October 2018, Sport For Jove will present *Ear to the Edge of Time* at Seymour. Recent book publications include *Dear Lindy* (National Library of Australia) and *Bowerbird: The art of making theatre drawn from life* (Currency Press). A jazz song cycle *Flight Memory* will be presented at The Street Theatre in Canberra late in 2018. Alana is currently co-recipient of a writing fellowship at the Charles Perkins Centre, University of Sydney.

SARAH GOODES Director

Sarah is an Australian theatre director recognised for bringing more than 12 new Australian works to the mainstage. She is currently Associate Director at Melbourne Theatre Company and was Resident Director at Sydney Theatre Company from 2013 to 2016. Her credits for Belvoir Downstairs include *The Sweetest Thing*, *The Small Things*, *Black Milk*, *Elling* and *The Italian American Reconciliation*. Other stage credits include *The Children*, *Switzerland* (Sydney Theatre Company/Melbourne Theatre Company); *John*, *Three Little Words* (Melbourne Theatre Company); *Disgraced*, *The Splinter*, *The Hanging*, *Battle of Waterloo* (Sydney Theatre Company); *The Effect* (Sydney Theatre Company/Queensland Theatre Company); *Vere* (Sydney Theatre Company/State Theatre Company of South Australia); *Edward Gant's Amazing Feats of Loneliness* (Sydney Theatre Company/La Boite); *The Schelling Point*, *Vertigo and the Virginia*, *Hilt*, *What Happened Was...* (Old Fitz); and *Scorched* (National Institute of Dramatic Art). Sarah's work has received multiple nominations for Helpmann Awards and Sydney Theatre Awards. Sarah is a graduate of both University of NSW majoring in Literature and Theatre (final year at San Diego at UCSD) and the Victorian College of the Arts (University of Melbourne) in Directing. Upcoming work includes directing *A Doll's House: Part II* starring Marta Dusseldorp, and *Astroman* for Melbourne Theatre Company.

Kris McQuade

Sheridan Harbridge & Josh McConville

DAMIEN COOPER Lighting Designer

Damien has designed more than 300 productions in dance, opera and theatre. For Belvoir, he has lit *Mark Colvin's Kidney*, *The Great Fire*, *Radiance*, *The Glass Menagerie*, *Coranderrk*, *Miss Julie*, *Stories I Want to Tell You in Person*, *Cat on a Hot Tin Roof*, *Private Lives*, *Conversation Piece*, *Neighbourhood Watch*, *The Seagull*, *Gethsemane* and *Keating!*. Other theatre highlights include *Exit The King* on Broadway, starring Geoffrey Rush and Susan Sarandon; *Cyrano de Bergerac*, *The Lost Echo*, *The Women of Troy*, *Peter Pan* (New Victory Theatre, New York). Opera design includes *The Ring Cycle* (Opera Australia); *A Midsummer Night's Dream* (Houston Grand Opera, Canadian Opera Company and Lyric Opera Chicago); *The Magic Flute* (Lyric Opera of Chicago); and *Aida*, *Cosi fan tutte*, *Peter Grimes* (Opera Australia and Canadian Opera Company). For The Australian Ballet, Damien's designs include Graeme Murphy's *Swan Lake*, presented in London, Paris, New York and Toyko, *The Narrative of Nothing*, *The Silver Rose*, *Romeo & Juliet*, *Firebird*, *Tivoli*. Damien has won three Sydney Theatre Awards for Best Lighting Design, three Green Room awards for Best Lighting Design and two Australian Production Design Guild awards for Best Lighting.

STEVE FRANCIS Composer

Steve has worked extensively in theatre, dance and screen. His Belvoir credits include *The Great Fire*, *Angels in America*, *This Heaven*, *Don't Take Your Love To Town*, *Babyteeth*, *The Book of Everything*, *The Power of Yes*, *Ruben Guthrie*, *Baghdad Wedding*, *Keating!*, *Paul*, *Parramatta Girls*, *Capricornia*, *Box the Pony*, *Gulpilil* and *Page 8*. His other theatre credits include *The Children*, *The Weir*, *The Sublime*, *Other Desert Cities* (Melbourne Theatre Company); *Still Point Turning*, *The Father*, *Talk*, *The Hanging*, *Disgraced*, *Orlando*, *Battle of Waterloo*, *Switzerland*, *After Dinner*, *Vere*, *Mojo*, *The Long Way Home*, *The Secret River*, *Machinal*, *Sex with Strangers*, *Travelling North*, *The Splinter*, *Bloodland*, *The White Guard* (Sydney Theatre Company); *Hamlet*, *Henry V* (Bell Shakespeare); and *A Rabbit for Kim Jong-il*, *Between Two Waves*, *This Year's Ashes*, *Speaking in Tongues* (Griffin). For dance, Steve has composed music for *Bennelong*, *Our Land People Stories*, *Lore*, *Belong*, *True Stories*, *Skin*, *Corroboree*, *Walkabout*, *Bush* and *Boomerang* (Bangarra Dance Theatre). Steve has also composed for film and TV. His awards include Best Original Score in 2012 and 2003 and Best New Australian Work in 2003 (Helpmann Awards), as well as Sydney Theatre Awards for Music and Sound in 2011 and 2014.

MICHAEL HANKIN Set Designer

Michael is a graduate of the National Institute of Dramatic Art (NIDA). He is a set and costume designer for theatre, dance, opera and film. His credits for Belvoir include *Hir*, *Ghosts*, *Mark Colvin's Kidney*, *Jasper Jones*, *My Urrwai*, *The Great Fire*, *Ivanov*, *The Glass Menagerie*, *Twelfth Night*, *The Dark Room*, *A Christmas Carol* and *Angels in America*. Some of his other theatre credits include *Memorial*, *The Aspirations of Daise Morrow* (Brink Productions); *Three Little Words* (Melbourne Theatre Company); *Jumpy* (Melbourne Theatre Company/Sydney Theatre Company); *Lake Disappointment* (Carriageworks); *The Merchant of Venice* (Bell Shakespeare); *Dirty Rotten Scoundrels* (Theatre Royal); *247 Days* (Chunky Move/Malthouse – Netherlands tour); *Tartuffe* (State Theatre Company of South Australia); *Songs for the Fallen* (Sydney Festival/New York Music Theatre Festival); *The Peasant Prince* (Monkey Baa); *You Animal You* (Force Majeure); *The Lighthouse*, *In The Penal Colony* (Sydney Chamber Opera); *Who's Afraid of Virginia Woolf* (Ensemble); and *Deathtrap* (Darlinghurst Theatre). Michael has been nominated for several Sydney Theatre Awards, winning Best Stage Design for *Hir*, Best Independent Stage Design for *Of Mice and Men* and *Truckstop*. He is the recipient of the 2018 Kristian Fredrikson Scholarship and was Associate Lecturer of Design at NIDA.

SHERIDAN HARBRIDGE Narelle Macreadie

Sheridan is an actor, playwright, singer and comedienne, graduating from the National Institute of Dramatic Art in 2006. Her work for Belvoir includes *The Dog/The Cat* and *Girl Asleep*. Other theatre credits include *Muriel's Wedding* (Sydney Theatre Company); *Kill Climate Deniers*, *Jump for Jordan* (Griffin); *North by Northwest*, *The Beast*, *The Speechmaker* (Melbourne Theatre Company); *Gaybies* (Darlinghurst); *80 Minutes No Interval* (Old Fitz); *Hip Bone Sticking Out*, *Blue Angel* (Big hArt); *Detective's Handbook*, *Calamity Jane*, *You're a Good Man Charlie Brown* (Hayes); and *Fiddler on the Roof*, *My Fair Lady* (Opera Australia). Her directing work includes *Nosferatutu*, *The Blueberry Play* (Griffin); and *Dahlesque* (Melbourne Symphony Orchestra). Her musical *Songs for the Fallen*, which has toured to major festivals around the world, won Best Musical and Outstanding Actress at the New York Music Theatre Festival in 2015, and a Green Room Award for Best Artist. She collaborated with UK cult band The Tiger Lillies for the Biennale, and appeared with John Cleese at the Just for Laughs Festival. She played Valerie Solanas and Judy Garland in Jim Sharman's film *Andy X*. TV credits include *Rake*, *All Saints*, *Wild Boys*, *Doctor Blake* and *The Justine Clarke Show*.

Sacha Horler

Kris McQuade & Lex Marinos

SACHA HORLER Margo Macreadie

Sacha is one of Australia's most loved and respected actors. Her theatre credits for Belvoir include *Peribanez*, *Blue Murder*, *The Birthday Party*, *Hamlet*, and *Svetlana in Slingbacks*. Sacha's other theatre credits include *Other Desert Cities* (Melbourne Theatre Company); and *Mariage Blanc*, *God of Carnage*, *The Removalists*, *The Crucible*, *Pygmalion*, *Three Sisters*, *Far Away*, *Life After George* (Sydney Theatre Company). This year Sacha stars in the title role in the ABC comedy series *Sando*, and on the big screen in *Peter Rabbit*. She has appeared in two award-winning Foxtel series', *The Kettering Incident* and *Secret City*, and opposite Kate Winslet in *The Dressmaker*, directed by Jocelyn Morehouse. Sacha's other screen work includes *The Letdown*, *The Moodys*, *Jack Irish*, *Catching Milat*, *Old School*, *Black Comedy*, *Beaconsfield*, *Hawke*, *Love My Way*, *Offspring*, *Rake*, *Small Time Gangster*, *Home and Away* and *A Few Less Men*. Sacha holds the rare distinction of winning two AFI awards on the one night: for lead role in *Praise* and supporting role in *Soft Fruit*. She won her third AFI award for best supporting actress in *Travelling Light*. She has also received AFI nominations for *My Year Without Sex*, *Secret Bridesmaids' Business*, *Russian Doll* and *Grass Roots*.

ISABELLA KERDIJK Stage Manager

Isabella graduated from the production course at the National Institute of Dramatic Art in 2008. She has worked as stage manager and assistant stage manager on many shows. Her work for Belvoir includes *Mother*, *My Name Is Jimi*, *HIR*, *The Dog/The Cat*, *Girl Asleep*, *The Drover's Wife*, *Jasper Jones*, *Mother Courage and Her Children*, *Kill the Messenger*, *The Glass Menagerie*, *20 Questions*, *Stories I Want to Tell You in Person* (national tour) and *Thyestes* (European tours). Isabella's other credits include *Replay*, *And No More Shall We Part*, *This Year's Ashes*, *Ugly Mugs* (Griffin); *Silent Night*, *Ride & Fourplay* (Darlinghurst); *Rainman*, *The Ruby Sunrise* (Ensemble Theatre); *Empire* (Spiegelworld); *Cranked Up* (Circus Oz); *The Mousetrap* (Australia/NZ tour – LWAA); and *Bubble* (Legs On the Wall). Isabella has worked as production coordinator on *Carmen* (Opera Australia on Sydney Harbour) and production manager/stage manager for *Puppetry of the Penis* (A-List Entertainment). She has also worked on various festivals including The Garden of Unearthly Delights, Sydney Festival and the Woodford Folk Festival.

LEX MARINOS Sidney Macreadie/Constable Rupert/Brian Tuckan/ Terence Sheahan

Lex was born in Wagga Wagga into a family of Greek cafe owners. He attended the University of NSW, receiving a Bachelor of Arts with Honours in Drama, and also studied with renowned American acting teacher, Stella Adler. He has worked in all areas of the entertainment industry as an actor, director, writer, broadcaster and teacher. He is best known for his television performances in *Kingswood Country* and *The Slap*, as well as numerous other series, and dozens of films and TV episodes. On stage, Lex has appeared with Nimrod, Belvoir, Australian Performing Group, Sydney Theatre Company, Melbourne Theatre Company, Big hART, and at many arts festivals, as well as commercial productions such as *The King and I*. His work has taken him all over Australia, from remote Indigenous communities to the Opening Ceremony of the 2000 Sydney Olympic Games. Lex has also worked extensively on ABC radio since the riotous inception of 2JJ. He has held many advisory and governance positions with arts and cultural organisations including SOCOG, the Australia Council, and Community Broadcasting Foundation. His book *Blood and Circuses: an irresponsible memoir* was published by Allen & Unwin. He is the recipient of an OAM, and has been a proud member of Actors Equity since 1970.

JOSH McCONVILLE Ollie Macreadie/Zee

Since graduating from the National Institute of Dramatic Art in 2008, **Josh**'s theatre credits include *All My Sons*, *A Midsummer Night's Dream*, *Arcadia*, *Hay Fever*, *After Dinner*, *Cyrano De Bergerac*, *Noises Off*, *Loot*, *In the Next Room*, *Cloud Nine*, *Gross Und Klein*, which also toured to Europe (Sydney Theatre Company); *The Boys*, *Dealing with Claire* (Griffin); *Death of a Salesman* (Black Swan Theatre Company); and *Hamlet* (Bell Shakespeare). Awards include *Noises Off* (Sydney Theatre Award for Best Supporting Actor), *The Boys* (Sydney Theatre Award for Best Actor in a Leading role) and Best Newcomer for *The Call* and *Strange Attractor* (Sydney Theatre Award). Josh's television credits include Southern Star's production of *Wild Boys*, Channel Nine's multi-award winning drama *Underbelly II: A Tale of Two Cities*, ABC's multi-award winning series *Redfern Now* and *Cleverman*, Channel Seven's *The Killing Field*, and *Home and Away*. His film credits include the lead role in *The Infinite Man*, as well as *The Turning: Commission* alongside Hugo Weaving and *Down Under*, directed by Abe Forsythe. Most recently, Josh can be seen in David Michôd's *War Machine* with Brad Pitt, and will appear as the lead in the new Australian war film *Escape and Evasion*, and alongside Ryan Corr in *1%*. *The Sugar House* is Josh's Belvoir debut.

KRIS McQUADE June Macreadie

Kris is a graduate of the National Institute of Dramatic Art. Select theatre credits for Belvoir include *Neighbourhood Watch*, *Strange Interlude*, *The Adventures of Snugglepot and Cuddlepie and Little Ragged Blossom*, *Our Lady of Sligo*, *Threepenny Opera* and *Cloudstreet* (including tours to Europe and the USA). Other theatre credits include *Maggie Stone* (State Theatre Company of South Australia); *Mourning becomes Electra* (Sydney Theatre Company); *Love Me Tender* (Griffin); *The Aspirations of Daise* Morrow, *When the Rain Stops Falling* (Brink Productions); and *The Odyssey* (Malthouse). Kris' recent television credits include roles in *Mystery Road*, *Rosehaven* (Series' 1 & 2), *The Kettering Incident* and *Wentworth* (Series 1). Film roles include *Cargo*, *Holding the Man*, *Subdivision*, *December Boys*, *Ned Kelly*, *Mullet*, *Better Than Sex* and *Strictly Ballroom*. Kris has received numerous awards and nominations for her work including AACTA, Logie and Equity Award nominations. Other acknowledgements include nominations for both Helpmann and Sydney Theatre Awards for *Neighbourhood Watch*, a Sydney Theatre Award nomination for *When the Rain Stops Falling* and a Helpmann Award nomination for *Cloudstreet*. Kris has received multiple AFI Award nominations, winning the Best Supporting Actress Award for her work on *Fighting Back*.

NIKKI SHIELS Jenny/Prin

Nikki last appeared for Belvoir in *The Rover* in 2017, and has previously appeared in *Twelfth Night*. For Malthouse Theatre Nikki recently reprised her role in *Picnic at Hanging Rock* which toured to the Barbican in the UK, and previously had an Edinburgh season at the Royal Lyceum Theatre. Other theatre credits include *Night On Bald Mountain*, *The Dragon* and *Elizabeth – Almost By Chance A Woman* (Malthouse); *Three Sisters* (Sydney Theatre Company); *The Unspoken Word is 'Joe'* (Griffin/La Mama); *The Dream* (Bell Shakespeare); *The Cherry Orchard*, *True Minds*, *Top Girls*, *Don Parties On* (Melbourne Theatre Company); *Joan* (The Rabble); *M + M* (Melbourne International Arts Festival); *The Dollhouse*, *Peer Gynt* (Daniel Schlusser Ensemble); *Madeleine* (Black Sequin Productions/Arts House); *Romeo and Juliet* (ZLMD Shakespeare Company); and *The Bitter Tears of Petra Von Kant* (Theatre Works/Dirty Pretty Theatre). Nikki's film and television credits include *Neighbours*, *House Husbands*, *Childhood's End*, *Rush IV* and Fred Schepisi's feature *The Eye of the Storm*.

Kris McQuade, Nikki Shiels
& Sheridan Harbridge

Lex Marinos

KEIREN SMITH Assistant Stage Manager

For Belvoir, **Keiren** has been stage manager on *Atlantis* and *La Traviata*, and assistant stage manager on *Single Asian Female*, *Hir*, *Mark Colvin's Kidney*, *The Drover's Wife*, *Back at the Dojo*, *Mother Courage and Her Children*, *Radiance*, *Nora*, *Brothers Wreck* and *Once in Royal David's City*. She has an Advanced Diploma in Stage Management from Western Australian Academy of Performing Arts and a Bachelor of Arts in Communication and Cultural Studies from Curtin University. Keiren was assistant stage manager with The Australian Ballet for three years, touring domestically and internationally including to Japan and New York, working on such productions as *Don Quixote*, *Onegin*, *The Merry Widow*, *Madame Butterfly*, *Coppelia*, *The Nutcracker*, *The Silver Rose*, Alexei Ratmansky's *Cinderella*, Stephen Bayne's *Swan Lake* and Graeme Murphy's *Romeo & Juliet*. She has stage managed *I Love You Now* (Darlinghurst); and was assistant stage manager on *Theodora* (Pinchgut Opera); *Hay Fever* (Sydney Theatre Company); *Solomon and Marion* (Melbourne Theatre Company); *The Web*, *Much Ado About Nothing* (Black Swan); and Sydney New Year's Eve – Lord Mayor's Party (City of Sydney).

MICHAEL TOISUTA Sound Designer

Michael has been sound designer at Belvoir on *Windmill Baby* and associate sound designer on *The Great Fire*, *Toy Symphony* and *Yibiyung*. Other theatre credits include *Flight Paths* (National Theatre of Parramatta); *Australian Graffiti* (Sydney Theatre Company); *Thicker than Water* (TerryandTheCuz); *Richard 3* (Bell Shakespeare); *Masquerade* (Griffin & State Theatre Company of South Australia); *All Good Things*, *Max Remy Super Spy* (Australian Theatre for Young People); *My Bicycle Loves You* (Legs on the Wall); *Framed* (DeQuincey Co); *Fracture* (New Ghosts & Old Fitz); and *Smudge* (The Kings Fools & Bakehouse). He has composed and sound designed for short films including *Dance Diaries: Home*, *Dance Diaries: Sydney* (Parramasala); *Double Landscape* (Bundanon Trust Siteworks); *Woodlands* (Barcelona International Film Festival); *Hairpin* (Dungog Film Festival); and *Jyoti* (Short Film Corner at Cannes Film Festival). He has also sound designed for the video art installation *Habitat* by Taloi Havini which exhibited as part of The National 2017 at the Art Gallery of New South Wales and at Palais de Tokyo in Paris, France.

EMMA VINE Costume Designer

Emma is a designer for theatre, opera, musical theatre, dance, television and film. Her theatre credits include *Turquoise Elephant*, *Sunset Strip* (Griffin); *Only Heaven Knows* (Hayes); *The Mystery of Love and Sex* (Darlinghurst); *Heathers: The Musical* (national tour); *The Waiting Room*, *Water Angel* (Sydney Opera House); *All Good Things: The Voices Project* (Australian Theatre for Young People); *Credeaux Canvas* (Seymour Centre); co-design of *Klutz* (Brisbane Festival, National Institute of Dramatic Art); *Three Sisters* (Sport for Jove); *Choreography*, *Kandahar Gate* (National Institute of Dramatic Art); and associate designer for *Anthony And Cleopatra* (Bell Shakespeare). Television credits include *Dead Lucky* (production design placement) and film credits include *Slam* (art department); short film, *Quietus* (production design), *The Fall* (costume design); and music video, *Into My Arms* (production design). Emma received Sydney Theatre Award nominations for best costume design in both 2017 and 2018 and was nominated as Best Emerging Designer at the 2017 Australian Production Design Guild Awards. Upcoming work includes set and costume design for *Jesus wants me for a Sunbeam* (National Theatre of Parramatta); *The Maids* and *The Overcoat* (25A Belvoir).

Nikki Shiels & Josh McConville

THEATRICALITY.
VARIETY OF LIFE.
FAITH IN HUMANITY.

Belvoir is a theatre company on a side street in Surry Hills, Sydney. We share our street with a park and a public housing estate, and our theatre is in an old industrial building. It has been, at various times, a garage, a sauce factory, and the Nimrod Theatre. When the theatre was threatened with redevelopment in 1984, over 600 people formed a syndicate to buy the building and save the theatre. More than thirty years later, Belvoir St Theatre continues to be home to one of Australia's most celebrated theatre companies.

In its early years Belvoir was run cooperatively. It later rose to international prominence under first and longest-serving Artistic Director Neil Armfield and continued to be both wildly successful and controversial under Ralph Myers. Belvoir is a traditional home for the great old crafts of acting and story in Australian theatre. It is a platform for voices that won't otherwise be heard. And it is a gathering of outspoken ideals. In short: theatricality, variety of life, and faith in humanity.

At Belvoir we gather the best theatre artists we can find, emerging and established, to realise an annual season of works – new Australian plays, Indigenous works, re-imagined classics and new international writing. Audiences remember many landmark productions including *The Drover's Wife, Angels in America, Brothers Wreck, The Glass Menagerie, Neighbourhood Watch, The Wild Duck, Medea, The Diary of a Madman, Death of a Salesman, The Blind Giant is Dancing, Hamlet, Cloudstreet, Aliwa, The Book of Everything, Keating!, The Exile Trilogy, Exit the King, The Sapphires, The Rover, Faith Healer* and many more.

Today, under Artistic Director Eamon Flack and Executive Director Sue Donnelly, Belvoir tours nationally and internationally, and continues to create its own brand of rough magic for new generations of audiences.

Belvoir receives government support for its activities from the federal government through the Australia Council and the state government through Create NSW. We also welcome and warmly appreciate all philanthropic support.

belvoir.com.au

BELVOIR STAFF

18 Belvoir Street, Surry Hills NSW 2010
Email mail@belvoir.com.au Web belvoir.com.au
Administration (02) 9698 3344 Facsimile (02) 9319 3165 Box Office (02) 9699 3444

Artistic Director
Eamon Flack
Executive Director
Sue Donnelly
Deputy Executive Director & Senior Producer
Aaron Beach

BELVOIR BOARD
Patricia Akopiantz (Deputy Chair)
Mitchell Butel
Luke Carroll
Sue Donnelly
Tracey Driver
Eamon Flack
Ian Learmonth
Michael Lynch
Sam Meers (Chair)
Stuart O'Brien
Peter Wilson

BELVOIR ST THEATRE BOARD
Stuart McCreery
Angela Pearman (Chair)
Sue Rosen
Nick Schlieper
Mark Seymour
Kingsley Slipper
Susan Teasey

ARTISTIC & PROGRAMMING
Artistic Associates
Tom Wright
Dom Mercer
Head of New Work
Louise Gough
Andrew Cameron Fellow
Carissa Licciardello
Artistic Administrator
Carly Pickard

EDUCATION
Education Manager
Jane May
Education Coordinator
Sharon Zeeman

FINANCE & OPERATIONS
Company Accountant
Barbara Lewis
Acting Finance Administrator
Shyleja Paul

MARKETING
Head of Marketing & Customer Service
Amy Goodhew
Marketing Coordinator
Georgia Goode
Communications Coordinator
Hilary Shrubb

BOX OFFICE & CUSTOMER SERVICES
Customer Experience & Ticketing Manager
Andrew Dillon
Ticketing Systems Administrator
Tanya Ginori-Cairns
Customer Service Coordinator
Anna Booty
Guest Operations Coordinator
Keila Terencio

FRONT OF HOUSE
House Manager, Venue & Events
Julie O'Reilly
Assistant Front of House Manager
Scott Pirlo

DEVELOPMENT
Philanthropy Managers
Joanna Maunder & Liz Tomkinson
Partnerships Manager
Julieanne Campbell
Development Coordinator
Kseniia Grishilova

PRODUCTION
Acting Production Manager
Ren Kenward
Technical Manager
Aiden Brennan
Deputy Production Manager
Roxzan Bowes
Senior Technician
Raine Paul
Resident Stage Manager
Luke McGettigan
Acting Staging & Construction Manager
Brett Wilbe
Staging & Construction Assistant
Emily Polson
Costume Coordinator
Judy Tanner

THE GROUP
Supporting *The Sugar House*

"Without wonder and insight, acting is just a trade. With it, it becomes creation." – Bette Davis

The Sugar House is The Group's first supported creation, a new Australian work written from the heart. With its rare combination of female writer (Alana Valentine), director (Sarah Goodes) and three extraordinary female lead roles (Kris McQuade, Sacha Horler and Sheridan Harbridge), this is the perfect project for The Group, a collective of like-minded women who are dedicated to supporting the great old craft of storytelling on stage.

The Group supports stories that address significant issues that affect women both locally and globally.

We'd like to see this grow.

So, join us and become part of this creative journey 'from page to stage', from development, to rehearsals, all the way to Opening Night!

You'd be standing with:

Patty Akopiantz
Catherine Brenner
Jillian Broadbent AO
Margaret Butler
Sally Cousens
Kate Donnelly
Holly Kramer
Robin Low
Sam Meers
Sarah Meers
Naomi O'Brien
Cecilia Ritchiei
Katriina Tahka
Cathy Yuncken

all of whom have been pivotal in making *The Sugar House* play come to life.

To find out how you can be part of this inspiring collective, contact our Development team on **02 8396 6209** or **development@belvoir.com.au**

Kris McQuade & Sheridan Harbridge

BELVOIR BRIEFINGS

Belvoir Briefings are your chance to hear directly from the artists about every show before it hits our stage.

For each production in 2018, the creative team will sit down to talk about why they wanted to tackle the story, how it's evolved in the rehearsal room, and what audiences can expect from the show. It's your ticket backstage.

Of course, there will also be time for you to ask your questions, and we'd love to continue the discussion in the bar afterward.

Belvoir Briefings are FREE but we'd like you to book online at **belvoir.com.au/events/belvoir-briefings** so we can save you a spot.

Bliss
6.30pm, Thursday 14 June

A Taste of Honey
6.30pm, Thursday 12 July

Calamity Jane
6.30pm, Thursday 9 August

An Enemy of the People
6.30pm, Thursday 27 September

The Dance of Death
6.30pm, Thursday 1 November

Sacha Horler

BELVOIR DONORS

We give our heartfelt thanks to all our donors for their loyal and generous support.

CHAIR'S CIRCLE
$10,000+
Patty Akopiantz & Justin Punch
Sophie & Stephen Allen
The Balnaves Foundation
Catherine & Philip Brenner
Anne Britton
Jillian Broadbent AO
Andrew Cameron AM &
Cathy Cameron
Roger Feletto
David Gonski AC & Associate
Professor Orli Wargon OAM
Anita Jacoby
Matthew & Veronica Latham
Ian Learmonth & Julia Pincus
Helen Lynch AM & Helen Bauer
Frank Macindoe
Nelson Meers AO & Carole Meers
Sam Meers & Richard Kuo
Catriona Mordant &
Simon Mordant AM
Cathie & Paul Oppenheim
Susanna & Matthew Press
Andrew & Andrea Roberts
Sherry-Hogan Foundation
Rob Thomas AM
Mark & Jacqueline Warburton
WeirAnderson Foundation
Kim Williams AM &
Catherine Dovey
Peter Wilson & James Emmett
Cathy Yuncken

CREATIVE
DEVELOPMENT FUND
$10,000+
Patty Akopiantz & Justin Punch
Sophie & Stephen Allen
Anne Britton**
Andrew Cameron AM
& Cathy Cameron***
Anita Jacoby*
Helen Lynch AM & Helen Bauer**
Frank Macindoe*
Cecilia Ritchie
Sherry-Hogan Foundation*
Shemara Wikramanayake
& Ed Gilmartin
Kim Williams AM &
Catherine Dovey**
Cathy Yuncken*

$5,000 – $9,999
Jill & Richard Berry
Hartley Cook**
Sue Donnelly & Michael Martin
Gail Hambly**
Louise Herron AM & Clark Butler**

Peter & Rosemary Ingle*
Don & Leslie Parsonage
Dan & Jackie Phillips
Doc Ross Family Foundation
Victoria Taylor**
$2,000 – $4,999
Neil Armfield AO**
Justin Butterworth
Anne & Michael Coleman*
Victoria Holthouse*
Richard, Heather & Rachel Rasker
Penelope Seidler AM
$500 – $1,999
Robert Crossman
Richard Evans
Ross McLean & Fiona Beith*
Louise & Michael Nettleton
Angela Pearman
Steve & Belinda Rankine
Sally & Jonathan Rourke
Penny Ward

B KEEPERS
$5,000+
Robert & Libby Albert***
Ellen Borda*
Constructability Recruitment
Marion Heathcote & Brian Burfitt**
Louise Christie**
Bruce Meagher & Greg Waters
Don & Leslie Parsonage*
Jann Skinner**
$3,000 – $4,999
Anonymous (1)
Suzanne & Michael Daniel**
Tom Dent
Bob & Chris Ernst**
Firehold Pty.Ltd.**
David & Kathryn Groves**
Judge Joe Harman
Michael Hobbs OAM**
Colleen Kane**
Tony Maxwell & Robyn Godlee
Chantal & Greg Roger***
Andrew & Lesley Rosenberg*
Peter & Jan Shuttleworth**
Merilyn Sleigh & Raoul de Ferranti
Patricia Wong
$2,000 – $2,999
Antoinette Albert**
Claire Armstrong & John Sharpe**
Max Bonnell**
Charlene & Graham Bradley AM
Chris Brown
Jan Burnswoods*
Jan Chapman &
Stephen O'Rourke***
Danny & Kathleen Gilbert**

Cary & Rob Gillespie
Sophie Guest**
Peter Graves***
David Haertsch***
John Head**
Libby Higgin*
Jennifer Ledgar & Bob Lim**
Professor Elizabeth More AM**
Dr David Nguyen**
Timothy & Eva Pascoe***
Richard, Heather & Rachel Rasker**
Michael Rose*
David & Emma Scambler
Ann Sherry AO*
Judy Thomson**
$1,000 – $1,999
Anonymous (3)
Cherry & Peter Best
Allen & Julie Blewitt
Jake Blundell
Mary Jo & Lloyd Capps***
Annabel Crabb & Jeremy Storer
Lisa Hamilton & Rob White
Wendy & Andrew Hamlin***
Avril Jeans**
Kevin & Rosemarie Jeffers-Palmer ***
Margaret Johnston***
A. le Marchant***
Ross McLean & Fiona Beith*
Stephanie Lee**
Atul Lele**
Hilary Linstead***
Louise McBride
Cajetan Mula (Honorary Member)
K Nomchong SC
Jacqueline & Michael Palmer
Greeba Pritchard*
Alex Oonagh Redmond**
Richmond Sisters
David Round
Jennifer Smith***
Chris & Bea Sochan**
Camilla & Andrew Strang
Sue Thomson*
Alese Watson
Paul & Jennifer Winch***

THE GROUP
$4,000+
Patty Akopiantz
Catherine Brenner
Jillian Broadbent AO
Margaret Butler
Sally Cousens
Kate Donnelly
Holly Kramer
Robin Low
Sam Meers
Sarah Meers

Naomi O'Brien
Cecilia Ritchie
Katriina Tahka
Cathy Yuncken

THE HIVE
$2,500
Elizabeth Allen & David Langley
Anthony & Elly Baxter
Aaron Beach & Deborah Brown
Nathan & Yael Bennett
Justin Butterworth
Dan & Emma Chesterman
Este Darin-Cooper & Chris Burgess
Joanna Davidson & Julian Leeser
Tracey Driver*
Piers Grove
Ruth Higgins & Tamson Pietsch
Hannah Roache & Luke Turner
Chris Smith
Peter Wilson & James Emmett*

EDUCATION DONORS
$10,000+
Doc Ross Family Foundation
Heather Doig & Rob Koczkar
Kimberly & Angus Holden
Susie Kelly
Ian Learmonth & Julia Pincus*
Nelson Meers Foundation
Rob Thomas AM

$5,000 - $9,999
Patty Akopiantz & Justin Punch
Ari and Lisa Droga
Veronica & Matthew Latham
Louise Mitchell & Peter Pether

$2,000 - $4,999
Anonymous (1)
Andrew Cameron AM &
Cathy Cameron**
Estate of the late Angelo Comino
Rowena Danziger AM
& Ken Coles AM
John B Fairfax AO & Libby Fairfax
Kiera Grant & Mark Tallis
Julie Hannaford*
Judge Joe Harman
David Jonas &
Desmon Du Plessis
Dan & Jackie Phillips

$500 - $1,999
Anonymous (8)
Len & Nita Armfield
Nicola Atkinson
AB*
Ian Barnett*
Brand New You
Dr Dee de Bruyn

Jessica Block
Andrew Bullock
John Campbell
Sue Capon
Denise & Robert Dunn
Joanna Elliott & David Ryan
Bob & Chris Ernst**
Susan Gabriel
Geoffrey & Patricia Gemmell*
Linda Herd
Dorothy Hoddinott AO**
Sue Hyde*
Peter & Rosemary Ingle*
Ruth Layton
Jennifer Ledgar & Bob Lim*
Christopher Matthies
Ruth Nicholas
Patricia Novikoff
Nicole Philps
Polese Family
Richard, Heather & Rachel Rasker
Angela Raymond
Ruth Ritchie
Stephen & Christy Roberts
Julianne Schultz
Margie Seale
Peter & Janet Shuttleworth*
Rob Sindel
Chris & Bea Sochan*
Dr Titia Sprague
Cheri Stevenson
Daniela Torsh
Catherine West & Julien Fouter
Ali Yeldham & Angus Hudson
Jason Yetton & Jo Lam
Ross Younsman
& Veronica Espaliat

GENERAL DONORS
$10,000+
Anonymous (1)
Andrew Cameron AM
& Cathy Cameron**
Ross Littlewood &
Alexandra Curtin*

$2,000 - $4,999
Anonymous (2)
Samantha Acret
Bill Hawker
Timothy & Eva Pascoe
Louisa Ward
Lynne Watkins & Nicolas Harding*

$500 - $1,999
Anonymous (9)
Annette Adair*
Victor Baskir*
Baiba Berzins*
Christine Bishop
Keith Bradley AM

Maxine Brenner
Anne Britton**
Robert Burns
Cadmium Property
Michael & Colleen Chesterman*
Darren Cook
Tim & Bryony Cox*
Jane Diamond*
Jane Mary Eagger
Anton Enus
Gillian Fenton
Sandra Ferman
Tim Gerrard
Verity Goitein
Peter Gray
Priscilla Guest*
Jill Hawker
Grania Hickley
Ruth Higgins
Elaine Hiley
Dorothy Hoddinott AO**
Robert Kidd
Cheryl L
Connie Liu
Elizabeth & Richard Longes
Lisa Manchur
Genie Melone
Irene Miller*
Peter Mitchell
Patricia Novikoff*
Judy & Geoff Patterson*
Christina Pender
Susan Pugh
David & Jill Pumphrey
Kim Rosser
Bernard Ryan & Michael Rowe
Leigh Rae Sanderson
Elfriede Sangkuhl
Rachel Scanlon
Chris & Bea Sochan*
Paul Stein
Leslie Stern
Mike Thompson*
Tom Tilley
Helen Trinca
Suzanne & Ross Tzannes AM*
Louise & Steve Verrier
Chris Vik & Chelsea Albert
Sarah Walters*
Louisa Ward
Elizabeth Webby AM*
Richard Willis
Brian & Trish Wright
Carolyn Wright

* 5+ years of giving   ** 10+ years
of giving   *** 15+ years of giving
List correct at time of printing.

BELVOIR DONORS Continued

Belvoir is very grateful to accept donations of all sizes. Donations over $2 are tax deductible. If you would like to make a donation or would like further information about any of our donor programs please call our Development Team on 02 9698 3344 or email development@belvoir.com.au

SPECIAL THANKS

We would like to acknowledge Cajetan Mula, Len Armfield and Geoffrey Scharer. They will always be remembered for their generosity to Belvoir.

We also thank our Life Members, who have made outstanding contributions to Belvoir over more than thirty years. They have changed the course of the company and are now ingrained in its fabric: Neil Armfield AO, Neil Balnaves AO, Andrew Cameron AM, David Gonski AC, Rachel Healy, Louise Herron AM, Sue Hill, Geoffrey Rush AC, Orli Wargon OAM and Chris Westwood.

These people and foundations supported the redevelopment of Belvoir St Theatre and purchase of our warehouse.

Andrew & Cathy Cameron
(refurbishment of theatre & warehouse)

Russell Crowe
(redevelopment of theatre)

The Gonski Foundation
& Nelson Meers Foundation
(Gonski Meers Foyer)

Andrew & Wendy Hamlin
(Executive Director's office)

Hal Herron
(The Hal Bar)

Geoffrey Rush
(redevelopment of theatre)

Fred Street AM
(Upstairs dressing room)

Baker McKenzie.

Proudly celebrating our support of Belvoir since 1994

www.bakermckenzie.com/australia

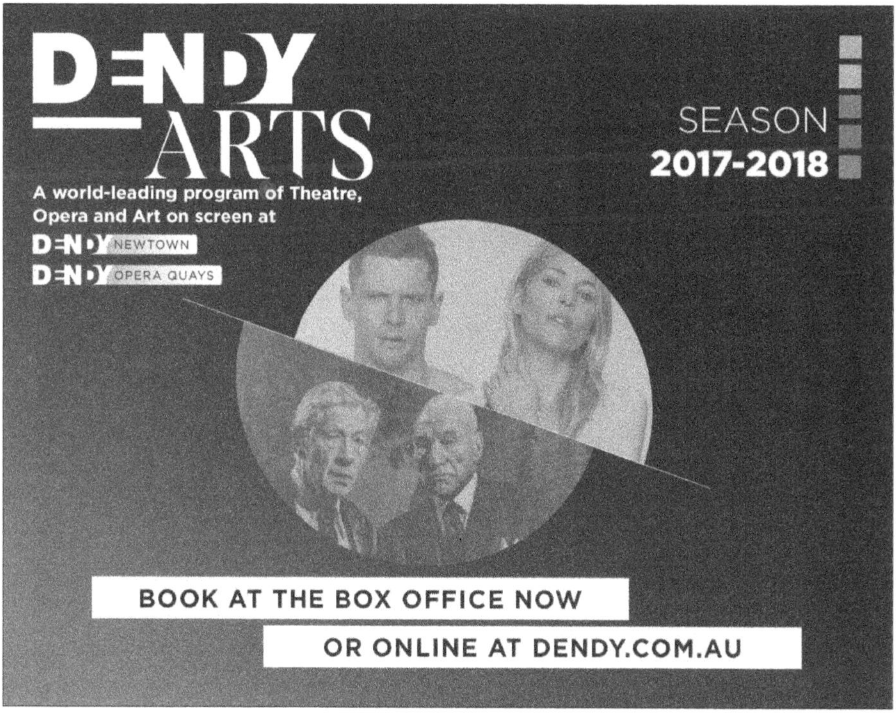

DENDY ARTS

A world-leading program of Theatre, Opera and Art on screen at

DENDY NEWTOWN
DENDY OPERA QUAYS

SEASON 2017-2018

BOOK AT THE BOX OFFICE NOW
OR ONLINE AT DENDY.COM.AU

HANDPICKED WINES

SYDNEY URBAN CELLAR DOOR
Your Destination for Australian Wine Education & Experiences

50 KENSINGTON STREET, CHIPPENDALE 2008 | www.handpickedwines.com.au | @handpickedwines

Thursday night food

From 7.30pm

SBS

#SBSFood

BELVOIR SUPPORTERS

Our patrons, supporters and friends are right there behind us, backing Belvoir in bringing to life the great old theatrical crafts of acting and storytelling. Thank you.

Learn more about supporting Belvoir at belvoir.com.au/support-belvoir

KEY SUPPORTER

Indigenous theatre at Belvoir supported by The Balnaves Foundation

TRUSTS & FOUNDATIONS

AMP Foundation
Andrew Cameron Family Foundation
Copyright Agency Cultural Foundation
Gandevia Foundation
The Greatorex Foundation
Macquarie Group Foundation
Nelson Meers Foundation
Teen Spirit Charitable Foundation
Thyne Reid Foundation
Walking up The Hill Foundation

BELVOIR PARTNERS

GOVERNMENT PARTNERS

YOUTH & EDUCATION PARTNER

MAJOR PARTNERS

ASSOCIATE PARTNERS

SUPPORTING PARTNER

MEDIA PARTNERS

IT PARTNER

PRODUCTION PARTNER

EVENT PARTNERS

For more information on partnership opportunities please contact our Development team on 02 9698 3344 or email development@belvoir.com.au

Correct at time of printing.

www.currency.com.au

Visit Currency Press' website now to:

- Order books
- Browse through our full list of titles including plays, screenplays, theory and reference/criticism, performance handbooks, educational texts and more
- Choose a play for your school or performance group by cast specs
- Seek performance rights
- Find out about performing arts news and sign up for our newsletter
- For students: read our study guides
- For teachers: access free curriculum information and teacher notes

We are also on Facebook and Instagram (@currencypress). Join the conversation!

The performing arts publisher

www.ingramcontent.com/pod-product-compliance
Lightning Source LLC
Chambersburg PA
CBHW050016090426
42734CB00021B/3293